ARE 4.0

Site Planning & Design

Paul Speiregen & Lester Wertheimer

with Contributing Editors Beatriz de Paz & Laura Serebin

MAHLUM

architects

KAPLAN AEC EDUCATION

President: Mehul Patel
Vice President & General Manager: David Dufresne
Vice President of Product Development and Publishing: Evan M. Butterfield
Editorial Project Manager: Jason Mitchell
Director of Production: Daniel Frey
Production Editor: Caitlin Ostrow
Production Artist: Cepheus Edmondson
Creative Director: Lucy Jenkins
Senior Product Manager: Brian O'Connor

Published by Kaplan AEC Education
30 South Wacker Drive, Suite 2500
Chicago, IL 60606-7481
(312) 836-4400
www.kaplanaecarchitecture.com

08   09   10   10   9   8   7   6   5   4   3   2

ISBN-13: 978-1-4277-7041-7

ISBN-10:   1-4277-7041-7

CONTENTS

INTRODUCTION

WELCOME

Thank you for choosing Kaplan AEC Education for your ARE study needs. We offer updates annually to keep abreast of code and exam changes and to address any errors discovered since the previous update was published. We wish you the best of luck in your pursuit of licensure.

ARE OVERVIEW

Since the State of Illinois first pioneered the practice of licensing architects in 1897, architectural licensing has been increasingly adopted as a means to protect the public health, safety, and welfare. Today, all U.S. states and Canadian provinces require licensing for individuals practicing architecture. Licensing requirements vary by jurisdiction; however, the minimum requirements are uniform and in all cases include passing the Architect Registration Exam (ARE). This makes the ARE a required rite of passage for all those entering the profession, and you should be congratulated on undertaking this challenging endeavor.

Developed by the National Council of Architectural Registration Boards (NCARB), the ARE is the only exam by which architecture candidates can become registered in the United States or Canada. The ARE assesses candidates' knowledge, skills, and abilities in seven different areas of professional practice, including a candidate's competency in decision making and knowledge of various areas of the profession. The exam also tests competence in fulfilling an architect's responsibilities and in coordinating the activities of others while working with a team of design and construction specialists. In all jurisdictions, candidates must pass the seven divisions of the exam to become registered.

The ARE is designed and prepared by architects, making it a practice-based exam. It is generally not a test of academic knowledge, but rather a means to test decision-making ability as it relates to the responsibilities of the architectural profession. For example, the exam does not expect candidates to memorize specific details of the building code, but requires them to understand a model code's general requirements, scope, and purpose, and to know the architect's responsibilities related to that code. As such, there is no substitute for a well-rounded internship to help prepare for the ARE.

4.0 Exam Format

The seven ARE 4.0 divisions are outlined in the table below.

DIVISION	QUESTIONS	VIGNETTES
Building Design & Construction Systems	85	Accessibility/Ramp Roof Plan Stair Design
Building Systems	95	Mechanical & Electrical Plan
Construction Documents & Services	100	Building Section
Programming, Planning & Practice	85	Site Zoning
Schematic Design	-	Building Layout Interior Layout
Site Planning & Design	65	Site Design Site Grading
Structural Systems	125	Structural Layout

The exam presents multiple-choice questions individually. Candidates may answer questions, skip questions, or mark questions for further review. Candidates may also move backward or forward within the exam using simple on-

ARCHITECTURAL HISTORY

Questions pertaining to the history of architecture appear throughout the ARE. The prominence of historical questions will vary not only by division but also within different versions of the exam for each division. In general, however, history tends to be lightly tested, with approximately three to seven history questions per division, depending upon the total number of questions within the division. One aspect common to all the divisions is that whatever history questions are presented will be related to that division's subject matter. For example, a question regarding Chicago's John Hancock Center and the purpose of its unique exterior cross bracing may appear on the Structural Systems exam.

Though it is difficult to predict how essential your knowledge of architectural history will be to passing any of the multiple-choice divisions, it is recommended that you refer to a primer in this field—such as Kaplan's *Architectural History*—before taking each exam, and that you keep an eye out for topics relevant to the division for which you are studying. It is always better to be overprepared than taken by surprise at the testing center.

screen icons. The vignettes require candidates to create a graphic solution according to program and code requirements.

Actual appointment times for taking the exam are somewhat longer than the actual exam time to allow candidates to check in and out of the testing center. All ARE candidates are encouraged to review NCARB's *ARE Guidelines* for further detail about the exam format, including recommended time allotment for each of the vignettes. These guidelines are available via free download at NCARB's Web site (*www.ncarb.org*).

Exam Format

It is important for exam candidates to become familiar not only with exam content, but also question format. Familiarity with the basic question types found in the ARE will reduce confusion, save time, and help you pass. NCARB has made practice software available that can be downloaded free of charge from their Web site. Candidates should download this software and become thoroughly familiar with its use.

The first and most common type is a straight-forward multiple-choice question followed by four choices (A, B, C, and D). Candidates are expected to select the correct answer. This type of question is shown in the following example.

> Which of the following cities is the capital of the United States?
>
> **A.** New York
>
> **B. Washington, DC**
>
> **C.** Chicago
>
> **D.** Los Angeles

The second type of question is a negatively worded question. In questions such as this, the negative wording is usually highlighted using all caps, as shown on page viii.

THE EXAM TRANSITION

ARE 3.1

In November 2005 NCARB released *ARE Guidelines* Version 3.1, which outlines changes to the exam effective February 2006. These guidelines primarily detailed changes for the Site Planning division, combining the site design and site parking vignettes as well as the site zoning and site analysis vignettes. For more details about these changes, please refer to Kaplan's study guides for the graphic divisions.

The guidelines mean less to those preparing for multiple-choice divisions. Noteworthy points are outlined below.

- All division statements and content area descriptions were unchanged for the multiple-choice divisions.

- The number of questions and time limits for all exams were unchanged.

- The list of codes and standards candidates should familiarize themselves with was reduced to those of the International Code Council (ICC), the National Fire Protection Association (NFPA), and the National Research Council of Canada.

- A statics title has been removed from the reference list for General Structures.

ARE 4.0

In the spring of 2007, NCARB unveiled ARE 4.0, available as of July 2008. According to NCARB, the 4.0 version of the exam will be more subject-oriented than 3.1, and is intended to better assess a candidate's ability to approach projects independently. The format combines the multiple-choice and graphic portions of different divisions, reducing the number of divisions from nine to seven.

The transition will be gradual, with a one-year overlap during which both ARE 3.1 and ARE 4.0 will be administered. Provided you pass at least one ARE 3.1 division prior to May 2008, you can continue to take ARE 3.1 divisions until July 2009.

If you have not passed all ARE 3.1 divisions by June 2009, you will be transitioned to the ARE 4.0 format. You will be given credit for ARE 4.0 divisions according to which 3.1 divisions you have passed. Visit *www.kaplanaecarchitecture.com* for more details.

In order to avoid being retested on subjects you have already passed, you should develop a strategy for which divisions you take in which order. Here are some key points to keep in mind:

- Building Technology is a key division in the transition; its vignettes will be dispersed across four ARE 4.0 divisions. Be sure to pass Building Technology if you have passed and want credit for any of the following ARE 3.1 divisions: Building Design/Materials & Methods; Construction Documents & Services; General Structures; Lateral Forces; or Mechanical & Electrical Systems.

- Pre-Design and Site Planning content will be shuffled in ARE 4.0: If you pass one, pass the other.

- General Structures, Lateral Forces, and the Structural Layout vignette from Building Technology are being merged into the Structural Systems division. If you pass any of these and want to avoid being retested on material you have already seen, pass all three.

Which of the following cities is NOT located on the west coast of the United States?

A. Los Angeles

B. San Diego

C. San Francisco

D. New York

The third type of question is a combination question. In a combination question, more than one choice may be correct; candidates must select from combinations of potentially correct choices. An example of a combination question is shown below.

Which of the following cities is/are located within the United States?

I.   New York

II.   Toronto

III. Montreal

IV.   Los Angeles

A. I only

B. I and II

C. II and III

D. I and IV

The single most important thing candidates can do to prepare themselves for the vignettes is to learn to proficiently navigate NCARB's graphic software. Practice software can be downloaded free of charge from their Web site. Candidates should download it and become thoroughly familiar with its use.

Recommendations on Exam Division Order

NCARB allows candidates to choose the order in which they take the exams, and the choice is an important one. While only you know what works best for you, the following are some general considerations that many have found to be beneficial:

1. The Building Design & Construction Systems and Programming, Planning & Practice divisions are perhaps the broadest of all the divisions. Although this can make them among the most intimidating, taking these divisions early in the process will give a candidate a broad base of knowledge and may prove helpful in preparing for subsequent divisions. An alternative to this approach is to take these two divisions last because you will already be familiar with much of their content. This latter approach likely is most beneficial when you take the exam divisions in fairly rapid succession so that details learned while studying for earlier divisions will still be fresh in your mind.

2. The Construction Documents & Services exam covers a broad range of subjects, dealing primarily with the architect's role and responsibilities within the building design and construction team. Because these subjects serve as one of the core foundations of the ARE, it may be advisable to take this division early in the process, as knowledge gained preparing for this exam can help in subsequent divisions.

3. Take exams that particularly concern you early in the process. NCARB rules prohibit retaking an exam for six months. Therefore, failing an exam early in the process will allow the candidate to use the waiting period to prepare for and take other exams.

EXAM PREPARATION

Overview

There is little argument that preparation is key to passing the ARE. With this in mind, Kaplan has developed complete learning systems that include study guides, practice vignettes, question and answer handbooks, and flash cards. This study guide offers a condensed course of study and will best prepare you for the exam when utilized along with the other tools in the learning system. The system is designed to provide you with the general background necessary to pass the exam and to provide an indication of specific content areas that demand additional attention.

In addition to the Kaplan learning systems, materials from industry-standard documents may prove useful for the various divisions of the ARE.

Course Method

This manual guides candidates through the Site Planning & Design division of the ARE by familiarizing you with the specifics of the test and reviewing simulated vignette problems. Following each vignette example is a suggested graphic solution, together with an analysis and explanation of how it evolved. Although other solutions are possible, the approach in every case consists of a logical sequence of steps that have proven successful over the years. The principal goal of this study aid is not to be a primer on design, but instead to teach an effective and methodical technique for approaching a difficult and unique examination. Candidates are encouraged to follow the logical process identified in this manual, step by step, in order to better understand the procedure required to successfully solve ARE vignette problems.

In addition to the vignette examples that are typical of the current ARE computerized test, actual NCARB vignettes from previous ARE exams, as well as a number of related exercise problems created by Kaplan AEC Education, are included. All of these examples are intended to prepare candidates as completely as possible for the Site Planning & Design graphic portion.

Preparation Basics

The first step in preparation should be a review of the exam specifications and reference materials published by NCARB. These statements are available for each of the seven ARE divisions to serve as a guide for preparing for the exam. Download these statements and familiarize yourself with their content. This will help you focus your attention on the subjects that are the focal point of each exam.

Prior knowledge of CAD or other graphic drawing programs is not necessary to successfully complete the exam. In fact, it is important for candidates familiar with CAD to realize they will experience significant differences between the drawing tools used in the ARE and the commercial CAD software used in practice.

While no two people will have exactly the same ARE experience, the following are recommended best practices to adopt in your studies:

Set aside scheduled study time.
Establish a routine and adopt study strategies that reflect your strengths and mirror your approach in other successful academic pursuits. Most important, set aside a definite amount of study time each week, just as if you were taking a lecture course, and carefully read all of the material.

Take—and retake—quizzes.
Take the quizzes that follow some lessons. The questions are intended to be straightforward and objective. Answers and explanations can be found in the back of the book. If you answer a question incorrectly, see if you can figure out why the correct answer is correct before reading the explanation.

Identify areas for improvement.
The quizzes allow you the opportunity to pinpoint areas where you need improvement.

Reread and take note of the sections that cover these areas and seek additional information from other sources. Use the question-and-answer handbook and online test bank as a final tune-up before taking the exam.

Take the final exam.

A final exam designed to simulate the ARE follows the last lesson of each study guide. Answers and explanations can be found on the pages following the exam. As with the lesson quizzes, retake the final exam until you answer every question correctly and understand why the correct answers are correct.

Use the flash cards.

If you've purchased the flash cards, go through them once and set aside any terms you know at first glance. Take the rest to work, reviewing them on the train, over lunch, or before bed. Remove cards as you become familiar with their terms. Review all the cards a final time before taking the exam.

Practice using the NCARB software.

Work through the practice vignettes contained within the NCARB software. You should work through each vignette repeatedly until you can solve it easily. As your skills develop, track how long it takes to work through a solution for each vignette.

Utilize the study guide.

After studying the materials in the study guide, practice solving the vignettes found at the conclusion of each lesson. The vignettes are intended to be straightforward and objective. Solutions and explanations can be found within the lessons. Pay special attention to the procedure used to work through each vignette.

Utilize the practice vignettes.

Additional practice vignettes can be found at the end of each lesson, allowing you the opportunity to practice working through different vignettes and pinpointing areas where you

need improvement. Reread and take note of the study guide sections that cover these areas and seek additional information from other sources. If you've purchased the practice vignettes, use them as a final tune-up for the exam.

Practice using the NCARB software.

Work through the practice vignettes contained within the NCARB software. You should work through each of these vignettes repeatedly until you can solve them fluently without any difficulty utilizing the software. As you develop your skills, keep track of how long it takes you to work through a solution for each one and note this for exam day.

Supplementary Study Materials

In addition to the Kaplan learning system, materials from industry-standard sources may prove useful for the various divisions of the ARE. Candidates should consult the list of exam references in the NCARB guidelines for the council's recommendations.

Test-Taking Advice

Preparation for the exam should include a review of successful test-taking procedures—especially for those who have been out of the classroom for some time. Following is advice to aid in your success:

Pace yourself.

Each division allows candidates at least one minute per question. You should be able to comfortably read and reread each question and fully understand what is being asked before answering. Each vignette allows candidates ample time to complete a solution within the time alloted.

Read carefully.

Begin each question by reading it carefully and fully reviewing the choices, eliminating those that are obviously incorrect. Interpret language literally, and keep an eye out for negatively worded questions. With vignettes, carefully review instructions and requirements. Quickly make a list of program and code requirements to check your work against as you proceed through the vignette.

Guess.

All unanswered questions are considered incorrect, so answer every question. If you are unsure of the correct answer, select your best guess and/or mark the question for later review. If you continue to be unsure of the answer after returning the question a second time, it is usually best to stick with your first guess.

Review difficult questions.

The exam lets you review and change answers within the time limit. Utilize this feature to mark troubling questions for review upon completing the rest of the exam.

Utilize reference materials.

Some divisions provide limited reference materials during the exam. These materials include formulas and other content that may prove helpful when answering questions. Note that candidates may not bring reference material with them to the testing center.

Best answer questions.

Many candidates fall victim to questions seeking the "best" answer. In these cases, it may appear at first glance as though several choices are correct. Remember the importance of reviewing the question carefully and interpreting the language literally. Consider the following example.

Which of these cities is located on the east coast of the United States?

A. Boston

B. Philadelphia

C. Washington, DC

D. Atlanta

At first glance, it may appear that all of the cities could be correct answers. However, if you interpret the question literally, you'll identify the critical phrase as "on the east coast." Although each of the cities listed is arguably an "eastern" city, only Boston sits on the Atlantic coast. All the other choices are located in the eastern part of the country, but are not coastal cities.

Remember that style doesn't count.

Vignettes are graded on their conformance with program requirements and instructions. Don't waste time creating aesthetically pleasing solutions and adding unnecessary design elements.

Don't kill the trees.

Most versions of the vignettes require that candidates avoid disturbing existing trees. Remember that any development that falls under the canopy of a tree will violate this requirement. Also remember that you can add trees to block wind or sun if you are unable to maintain the ideal orientation of your solution.

Use sketch lines.

The ARE software allows you to draw sketch lines while creating your solution. You can use these lines to serve as guides while laying out setbacks, clearances, and element locations before final placement.

Pay close attention to directions.

When reading the program requirements, note the difference between words such as "near" versus "adjacent" or "should" versus "shall." In each case, the former gives you more flexibility than the latter.

Align driveways properly.

Keep driveways perpendicular to streets. The site planning vignettes nearly always require perpendicular intersections.

Accuracy and tolerances.

Candidates are responsible for being as accurate as possible when drawing their solution. Using the zoom, full screen cursor, and background grid features in the NCARB software will make it easier to produce more accurate solutions. Additionally, a check tool is available in several of the vignettes to identify overlapping elements and other problems.

Although tolerances are built into each scoring program to allow for slight inaccuracies, these tolerances vary from vignette to vignette based on the importance of the feature being evaluated. In general, whenever a specific programmatic requirement is noted in the exam instructions, candidates should be careful to meet that criteria as closely as possible.

ACKNOWLEDGMENTS

This course was written and illustrated by Lester Wertheimer, FAIA. Mr. Wertheimer is a licensed architect in private practice in Los Angeles and a founding partner of Architect Licensing Seminars. For many years he has written and lectured throughout the country on the design aspects of the ARE.

Portions of this edition were revised by Bob J. Wise, Jr., AIA. Bob is a technical director for A. Epstein & Sons International in San Antonio, Texas. He has led ARE review seminars for the San Antonio chapter of the American Institute of Architects for several years, and is a former member of NCARB's exam writing and scoring committees. Bob is also senior lecturer in the School of Architecture at the University of Texas at San Antonio. He led an ARE review session for the Site Planning division at the 2006 AIA national convention.

Special thanks to Thomas Wollan for his contributions to previous updates.

The introduction to this study guide was written by John F. Hardt, AIA. Mr. Hardt is vice president and senior project architect with Karlsberger, an architecture, planning, and design firm based in Columbus, Ohio. He is a graduate of Ohio State University (MArch).

ABOUT KAPLAN

Thank you for choosing Kaplan AEC Education as your source for ARE preparation materials. Whether helping future professors prepare for the GRE or providing tomorrow's doctors the tools they need to pass the MCAT, Kaplan possesses more than 50 years of experience as a global leader in exam prep and educational publishing. It is that experience and that history that Kaplan brings to the world of architectural education, pairing unparalleled resources with acknowledged experts in ARE content areas to bring you the very best in licensure study materials.

Only Kaplan AEC offers a complete catalog of individual products and integrated learning systems to help you pass all seven divisions of the ARE. Kaplan's ARE materials include study guides, mock exams, question-and-answer handbooks, video workshops, and flash cards. Products may be purchased individually or in division-specific learning systems to suit your needs. These systems are designed to help you better focus on essential information for each division, provide flexibility in how you study, and save you money.

To order, please visit *www.KaplanAEC.com* or call (800) 420-1429.

Part I

The Multiple-Choice Exam

MOVEMENT AND UTILITY SYSTEMS

INTRODUCTION

The usefulness of any parcel of land, whether urban, suburban, or rural, depends on the existence of adequate roads and utilities to serve it. This holds true for a small suburban site as well as a large urban one. Regardless of its other advantages, land is of little value for any kind of development if it is not readily accessible, or if it cannot be serviced by the various required utilities. People must be able to come to a site, move about it, and be able to perform all those functions that the various utility systems support. A primary consideration in planning the use of a site, therefore, includes the adequacy of both circulation access and utility services. Circulation access includes pedestrian, vehicular, and public transit movement systems; utility services include water, sewer, gas, electricity, and communication systems. Sustainable design planning attempts to design infrastructure and utilities that work with the natural ecosystems. Locating the infrastructure (roads, drainage, etc.) in locations that complement existing conditions creates designs that sympathetically—and more uniquely—reflect the local topography, climate, and vegetation.

CIRCULATION SYSTEMS

In land planning as well as site planning, it is convenient and useful to begin with the layout of the surface road systems, since they most often determine the patterns of land use and utility systems. Road systems must be carefully adapted to the topography. They also occupy a considerable amount of surface area. Utility services are generally located above and/

or below the road system. Surface drainage channels are often located alongside roadways, connecting to underground storm water conduits. Pedestrian walkways are also frequently located alongside or parallel to roadways. Thus, vehicular circulation systems are a primary structuring element of a land use plan, often determining the location of utility and communication networks and pedestrian circulation systems.

There are certain characteristics basic to all circulation systems. As the amount of vehicular or pedestrian flow increases, the need to organize and define the channels of flow also increases. As a result they must be carefully integrated into the network of local circulation routes. Those channels that carry large volumes over greater distances are often physically separated from the region served. Expressways, freeways, and railroads are examples of this separation. Urban circulation must utilize all possible means of transport available: individual auto, public transit, and truck or rail (if possible) for moving goods.

The forms of circulation networks have evolved as grid, radial, linear, or curvilinear systems, as well as combinations of these.

The *grid system* consists of equally spaced streets or roads which are perpendicular to each other. This system is often used because of its regularity, simplicity, and convenience. The grid system simplifies the subdivision of land for both agricultural and urban use, as well as affording a sense of orientation, if it is not used too extensively and if it contains sufficient orienting landmarks. Of course, it is well suited to level ground, but it can also be adapted, with care, to sloping ground. Grids can be used for complex distributions of flow, provided a hierarchy of flow channels is established. Traffic flows may be controlled by increasing capaci-

ties in certain channels while decreasing them in others, thereby directing heavier through-traffic to those channels that are capable of handling them. A grid system need not consist of straight lines nor need it enclose blocks of equal size or shape. If a proper hierarchy of flow is established, the grid can provide great efficiency of movement and ease of orientation without necessarily being monotonous or ignoring the natural topography of an area. A grid pattern loses its usefulness, as far as circulation is concerned, when its main traffic channels become congested. Before this point is reached, however, an expressway or freeway system is often introduced, relieving local streets of high-speed through-traffic.

The *radial system* directs flow to or from a common center, with straight channels of circulation radiating from this center point. Radial systems are the patterns that circulation routes assume as cities grow outward (radially) from small settlements. As growth occurs, so does congestion of the center, where the radial routes converge. To alleviate that congestion the center can be expanded in a linear direction. Or a series of by-passes connecting outlying radials can be created, thereby allowing through-traffic to skirt the center. Cumulatively, these by-passes become a "beltway," and the system forms a radio-centric circulation pattern. Another possibility is the formation of outlying sub-centers, which are the hubs of new radial and subsequently, radiocentric patterns. Sometimes a series of concentric or ring routes develops.

The *linear system* of circulation connects flow between two points, either along a single line or along a series of parallel lines. Various activities are located along the linear route which may, in order to ease localized movement, be routed into loops or branches on either or both of its sides. Excessive traffic moving along such a route may, of course, result in congestion. Other potential drawbacks to this system are that it does not develop a particular focal point and that the numerous off-and-on movements along its length can impede the smooth flow of traffic. Not only does this reduce its carrying capacity or efficiency, it is also dangerous. Nevertheless, it is useful where development is restricted by natural topography, as in a narrow valley, or where development parallels an existing transportation artery such as a railroad, canal, or freeway. Such routes, lined with businesses, are often referred to as "strip commercial" developments. They are a common outgrowth of urban expansion into the developing suburban countryside. They are, most often, visually chaotic, and quite inefficient in terms of land use. However, they furnish a large amount of commercial "incubator" (new business) space.

The *curvilinear system* responds to the topography of land and aligns with natural contours. This is a desirable form at a small scale, where it results in reduced traffic speeds. A network of curvilinear streets can form a pattern that is responsive to natural topography, and so in harmony with the landscape. A curvilinear system can also be used insensitively, simply as an abstract pattern. This has often been done in residential suburbs. However, many planned residential developments (PUDs) employ this system because of the potential for more interesting street layouts, better views, and adaptability to topographic changes.

The planner must determine the best possible system for a given set of conditions; however, in all cases, the system selected must be compatible with the overall pattern of circulation of the surrounding region.

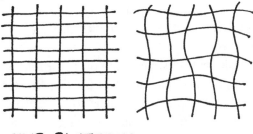

GRID PATTERNS

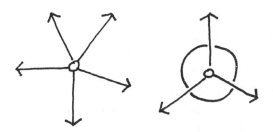

RADIAL PATTERNS

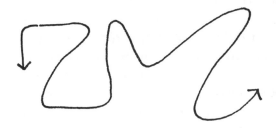

CURVILINEAR PATTERN

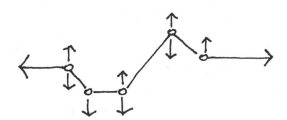

LINEAR PATTERN WITH BRANCHES
Figure 1.1

Vehicular Circulation

The development potential of land is largely determined by the system of traffic access to the land. The internal network of streets establishes movement patterns and subdivides the remaining land into development parcels.

The planner must be aware of the problems in gaining convenient and safe access to a particular site, in relation to the uses to which the site will be put. For example, the placement of a regional shopping center in the heart of a residential development would place an inordinate burden on local streets, by creating severe problems of congestion as well as safety. Thus, it is necessary to determine carrying capacities and appropriate types of traffic for different types of streets. An understanding of the classification and patterns of urban roadways, then, is essential to make such determinations. The basic categories of traffic arteries are: (1) freeways, expressways, or motorways, (2) arterial streets or highways, (3) collector-distributor streets, and (4) local access streets.

Freeways (expressways) are designed to allow movement of large volumes of traffic between, around, or through urban centers. Vehicles move at more rapid speeds because access to and egress from expressways are limited and occur at greater intervals to prevent speed reduction and abet safety. Crossings of traffic flow are handled by overpasses or underpasses, thus eliminating all grade-level intersections, which would impede flow. Grades, curves, lane widths, directional signs, road surfaces, on-and off-ramps, and limited access to adjacent property along expressways are designed for safety and rapidity of large-volume movement.

Arterial streets are continuous vehicular channels that connect with expressways by means of on- and off-ramps at carefully determined locations. These streets are typically two to three lanes wide in each direction. Parking is not normally allowed; direct access to adjacent commercial property may be restricted while access to residential streets is provided. Grade-

level vehicular and pedestrian crossings are controlled by traffic signals. Most areas impose speed limits of about 35 mph on such streets.

Collector-distributor streets serve as the transition between arterial streets and the local access streets of neighborhoods. They provide access to adjacent residential properties. These streets are frequently discontinuous, thereby preventing through-traffic and reducing vehicle speeds. Curbside parking is usually allowed; however, under certain conditions and during specific times of the day, parking may be limited or prohibited. Although intersections with arterial streets are normally controlled by traffic signals, local access street intersections may have only stop signs. Pedestrians are accommodated by sidewalks and crosswalks.

Local access streets provide access to low-intensity uses fronting on them. They carry low traffic flows. Such streets often have the form of loops, cul-de-sacs, or combinations of the two. They allow unrestricted pedestrian use. Minimum allowable vehicle speeds prevail, and curbside parking is unrestricted.

Vehicular traffic flows in sequential order, from low intensity to high intensity. Local access streets lead to the collector-distributor streets, on which are located local centers, small scale activities, and moderate density housing developments. Collector-distributor streets lead to arterial streets, which are designed to carry heavy traffic flows, with intersections and crossings located at longer intervals, more intensive uses, and access controlled but not excluded. From the arterial roads, vehicles have access to expressways (freeways), where grade-separated intersections are widely spaced, and fronting access does not occur.

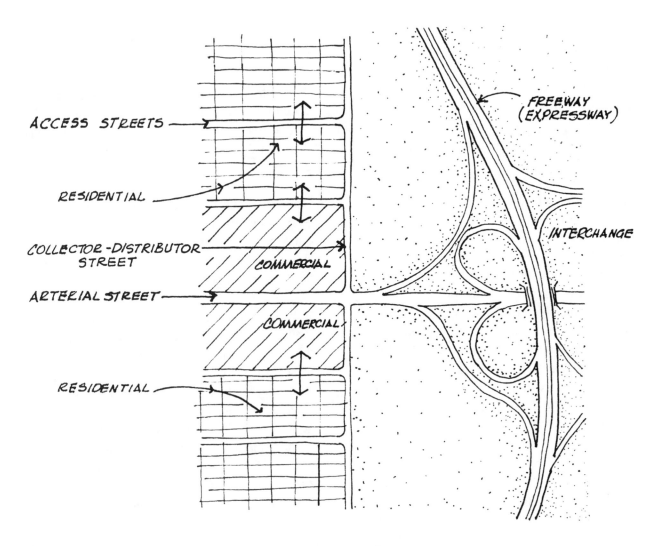

CLASSIFICATION OF TRAFFIC ARTERIES

Figure 1.2

Design Criteria

The cross section of a street or road normally remains constant. The cross section refers to the detailed street or road design, and includes such elements as pavement, curbs, gutters, shoulders, walks, landscaped border strips, lighting, signs, traffic signals, and utilities. The paved vehicular right-of-way usually slopes from a high point at the center, known as the crown, to the sides at a rate of 1/8 to 1/2 inch per foot, depending upon the finished surface, to provide positive drainage.

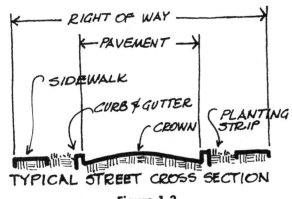

TYPICAL STREET CROSS SECTION

Figure 1.3

Streets with heavier traffic loads are designed with a six-inch curb and gutter. On minor residential streets, it may be sufficient to have four-inch "roll curbs" or simple gravel shoulders flanked by narrow drainage devices.

Depending on traffic intensities, the materials most often employed for paving streets and roads include, in order of preference: concrete, asphaltic concrete, gravel, decomposed granite, stabilized soil, and graded and compacted earth shaped for drainage.

Street widths are determined by the number of traffic and parking lanes to be provided. Widths of traffic lanes for individual vehicles for major roads vary from 11 to 12 feet. A typical two-lane highway, allowing nine feet for shoulders on each side, is therefore 40 to 42 feet wide. Parking lanes are eight feet wide for parallel parking and 2 to 2 1/2 times that dimension for angled or perpendicular parking.

A landscaped strip is often used to separate a street from an adjacent sidewalk. The planting strip can accommodate street trees as well as utilities and lighting fixtures. Such a strip must be at least seven feet wide if it is to contain trees, and four feet if it is landscaped with ground cover only. To allow for greater foot traffic in commercial areas, paving may extend to the curb, eliminating the planting strip. In such cases trees may be located in tree wells, and planting may be provided in raised planters.

Road alignment must be designed to conform to the natural topography of an area. All route patterns require variation in grade, both to accommodate to topography and to provide proper surface drainage. Indeed, the larger the area for which a road system is being planned, the greater the likelihood that the planner will have to design a series of horizontal and vertical curves. This requires the services of a civil engineer. However, the planner must be familiar with the basic concepts of road design.

A hypothetical center line is used as a reference in describing the alignment of a road. Actual roads consist of straight sections called "tangents," which may or may not be level, and curves.

Horizontal curves generally are arcs of a circle, enabling a driver of a vehicle to negotiate the curve smoothly and easily, since a turn of the steering wheel creates a circle if the wheel is held in a fixed position.

In laying out the road horizontally, certain practices are commonly followed: (1) two curves in the same direction (broken-back curves) should be separated by a tangent not less than 200 feet long, (2) two curves in opposite directions (reverse curves) should be separated by a tangent not less than 100 feet long, (3) two curves in the same direction with different radii (compound curves) should be avoided altogether, (4) simple curves, where a circular arc connects tangents at each end, may employ tangents of any length.

Vertical road alignment also involves curves, but in this case the curves are parabolic (flattened) rather than circular. Good vertical alignment provides a comfortable transition between two different grades, avoiding overly steep inclines, sudden bumps, and hollows. A minimum of variations in grade is highly desirable, but this objective must be tempered by consideration of the costs involved in extensive regrading. Freeways, for example, may require considerable cutting and filling, which is expensive and which requires extensive reshaping of the landscape. But this is the cost of a proper and safe high-speed road. Quite simply, the greater the intensity of traffic flow, the greater the necessity for minimizing sudden changes in grade.

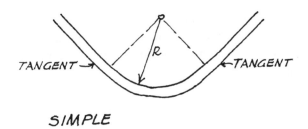

SIMPLE

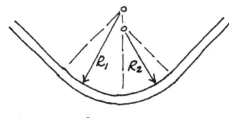

100 FOOT MINIMUM
TANGENT

REVERSE

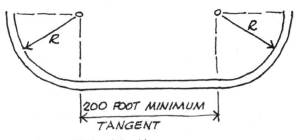

COMPOUND

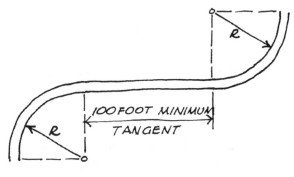

200 FOOT MINIMUM
TANGENT

BROKEN BACK

HORIZONTAL ROAD ALIGNMENT
Figure 1.4

Horizontal and vertical curves allow the designer to fit a road to existing topography, while taking advantage of natural site features and maintaining economy in design. Good road design attains a balance between curvature and

grade to provide smooth traffic flow. There are no sudden variations in alignment. Sight distances are kept long, to maintain a relatively distant forward view for the driver. In order to study the appearance of a road design in three dimensions, and as experienced by a driver, designers may build scale models or utilize computer graphics for visualization. Properly designed roads are safe, efficient, and visually interesting.

A serious consequence of poor road design is the danger of improperly located intersections. The design, with the assistance of a traffic engineer, must analyze road intersections with regard to potential conflicts between vehicles approaching from different directions, as well as between vehicles and pedestrians. There are certain types of intersections which should be avoided. An acute angle intersection (where the angle between the intersecting streets is less than 80° to 85°) is difficult to negotiate and limits driver visibility. Intersections that are slightly offset create two problems: (1) it is very difficult for the cross traffic to negotiate the intersection, and (2) the movement of traffic along the road being crossed is impeded. Intersections in a straight line, or those offset by no less than 150 feet, are safer and provide a smoother flow of traffic. Intersections on major arterial roads should be separated at least 800 feet. Freeway on- and off-ramps are normally spaced from one-half to one mile apart. On minor roads, where direct crossings are of lesser consequence, "T" intersections are permissible.

There are some rules of thumb in the design of street and road systems, that can be employed as basic standards, allowing for variations. Some of these are as follows:

The length of a cul-de-sac should not exceed 400 feet. A minimum turnaround at the end of a cul-de-sac should be provided which is at least 80 feet in diameter and free of parking.

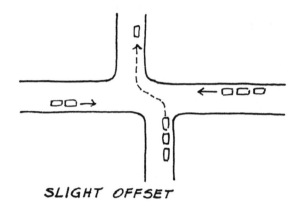

SLIGHT OFFSET

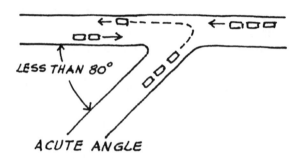

ACUTE ANGLE

UNDESIRABLE TRAFFIC INTERSECTIONS
Figure 1.5

Maximum depth of loop streets is 700 feet. The maximum length of a block is 1,600 feet. Curb radii at minor street intersections should be 12 feet minimum, and at major streets 50 feet minimum, in order to allow for ease of turning. Movement control systems are of equal importance in the design of intersections. Control devices include stop signs, traffic signals, turning lanes, islands, medians, and grade separations. When the intersection volume exceeds 750 vehicles per hour, traffic signals are employed.

Grade separations, which are warranted when traffic volume exceeds 3,000 vehicles per hour, are the most expensive and space-consuming types of intersections. They must be clearly marked and identified by signs to avoid confusion. Interchange structures are permanent and provide little opportunity for change in the future.

The most common grade-separated intersection is the cloverleaf. This configuration is based on a system of right turns.

The direct left-turn interchange may be used where two expressways intersect. This configuration is more complex and expensive than a cloverleaf, but it allows more lanes to operate at high speed in all changes of direction.

Diamond intersections are used where expressways intersect secondary roads. These are economical and use relatively little space. The critical design elements for these intersections are ramp grades, turning radii, and lengths of the acceleration and deceleration lanes. Up-ramp slopes are usually between 3 and 6 percent; down ramps, 8 percent.

Parking

Parking constitutes a major land use in itself. Parking areas that are poorly placed in relation to natural topography or to the various uses of a site are visually and functionally disruptive. All types of contemporary site and land uses require that a considerable portion of a site be allocated to parking. Consequently, consideration must be given to storing the required number of vehicles, as well as their safe movement while traversing the site.

The location of a parking area in relation to a building, or group of buildings, should also be given careful consideration. An approaching driver should have a view of the building, if possible, not a view of a larger parking area. A desirable arrangement is to locate the on-site approach drive between the building and the parking area, providing a clear view of the building entrance. An approaching driver then knows where to enter the building, and searches for a convenient parking stall.

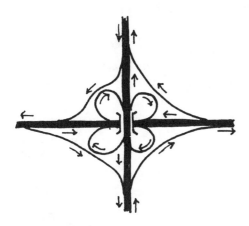

CLOVERLEAF

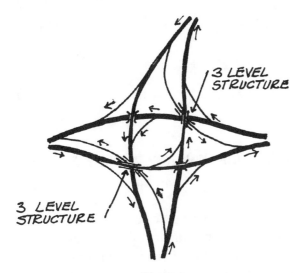

3 LEVEL STRUCTURE

3 LEVEL STRUCTURE

DIRECT LEFT-TURN INTERCHANGE

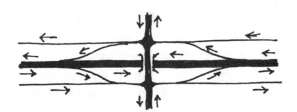

DIAMOND INTERCHANGE

GRADE SEPARATED INTERSECTIONS

Figure 1.6

As parking lots become larger, the problem of receiving and distributing entering automobiles, as well as enabling departing automobiles to disperse, becomes more acute. This becomes critical when the number of cars exceeds 400 to 500. For such large numbers of cars, it is necessary to design an on-site circulation system, carefully connected to the local public road system. A commonly used and effective design is an on-site loop distributor-collector drive with carefully located access points to the local road system. This is essential for the parking areas of large shopping centers. Such loops are often termed "cartridge roads," which describes their function in receiving or dispersing cars one at a time.

In order to organize parking, the designer must be aware of the dimensional and movement characteristics of vehicles. The dimensions to be considered include: vehicle length (bumper to bumper), width, and front and rear overhang length. Turning radii for both inside and outside front and rear bumpers must be known. Where a mixture of vehicles is anticipated (cars, buses, trucks), the design must consider the largest vehicle to be accommodated. The considerable dimensional differences between full-size, compact, and sub-compact cars should be taken into consideration in design layout, if possible.

All parking areas, in surface as well as structured parking, must provide clearly marked reserved parking for handicapped persons. These must be located near building entrance points, and designed to allow unimpeded movement by handicapped persons. The number of such spaces and their dimensions are normally specified in codes for handicapped access. Older parking areas must often be retrofitted to provide handicapped parking.

It may also be wise to provide parking by bicycles and motorcycles, depending on local usage.

8'-4" is a reasonable minimum width for a typical parking stall. This allows 20 inches of clearance between full-size cars when these are centered in the stalls. With this clearance, most car doors reach the first stop position without touching the adjacent vehicles. For parking angles less than 40 degrees, stall width may be reduced to 8 feet, since car doors can be opened without touching adjacent vehicles. Stalls are generally 18 to 20 feet long, depending on the size of vehicle to be accommodated.

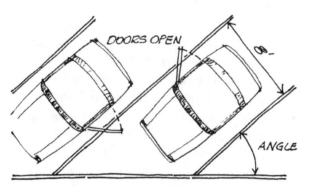

PARKING ANGLES LESS THAN 40°
Figure 1.7

Parking aisles may serve one-way or two-way traffic, depending on the layout. The width of the parking aisle is determined by the maneuvering space required to get in and out of the stalls. The minimum desirable width of a one-way circulation aisle is 12 feet. Based on this, the minimum bay widths for angle parking with one-way aisles are as follows:

Parking Angle	Projection	Bay Width
30 degrees	15'-7"	43'-2"
35 degrees	16'-7"	45'-2"
40 degrees	17'-6"	47'-0"
45 degrees	18'-2"	48'-4"

Two-way parking aisles serve parking stalls on either side of the aisle. The stalls may be angled for traffic moving in opposite directions, or they may be at 90 degrees.

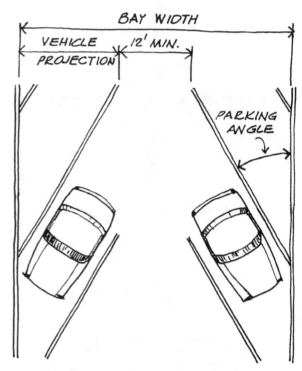

DETERMINATION OF PARKING BAY WIDTH
Figure 1.8

For 90-degree parking, the aisle width is determined by the amount of maneuvering space required to get in and out of the stall. For 90-degree parking, the total width of the two 90-degree stalls plus the two-way aisle varies from 60 feet (for 9'-0" wide stalls) to 64 feet (for 8'-4" wide stalls). At very flat stall angles (up to 50 degrees) aisle width is determined by the acceptable driveway width for two-way through traffic. This is normally a minimum of 20 feet between vehicle projections. Tighter standards can be maintained in attendant parking systems because of the attendants' familiarity with the facility. Stalls 8 feet by 18 feet and aisles 20 feet wide for 90-degree parking are considered to be minimum under such circumstances.

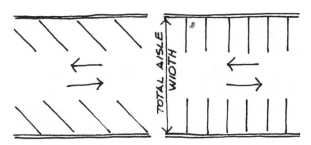

TWO-WAY PARKING AISLES
Figure 1.9

In estimating total area needs, it is advisable to allow 400 square feet of parking area per vehicle. Furthermore, the designer should be aware of accepted parking ratio standards. For example, shopping centers require 3,000 to 4,000 square feet of parking for every 1,000 square feet of tenant space.

By way of further example, an office building may have one parking space for every 350 to 400 gross square feet of floor area. This usually provides sufficient space for both visitor and tenant parking, depending on the type of occupancy of the building. Such ratios are normally specified in zoning ordinances.

The designer must be aware of some of the basic characteristics of parking systems. For example, more cars can be parked at 90 degrees, using the same stall width dimension, than at either 60 or 45 degrees. On the other hand, 60, 45, and 30-degree layouts establish a one-way circulation system, and they are easier for a driver to maneuver a vehicle into or out of. However, it is more convenient and less dangerous to back out of a space at 90 degrees because of the greater aisle width.

Acute angle parking occupies more area because of the curb length of each stall, its length, and the triangular area at the end of each stall which is wasted.

Should changes in grade levels be required, ramps should not be steeper than 15 percent. For slopes over 10 percent, a transition of at least eight feet in length should be provided at each end of the ramp at one-half the slope of the ramp itself.

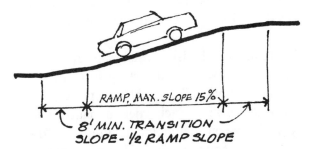

AUTO RAMP CRITERIA
Figure 1.10

A ramped driveway exit rising up to a public sidewalk must have a transition section that is nearly level (no more than 5 percent) before intersecting the sidewalk, to prevent the hood of the car from obscuring the driver's view of pedestrians on the walk.

Parking areas should be sloped to provide proper drainage. The slope should be at least 1 percent, but no greater than 5 percent. Circulation within parking areas should be continuous, the number of turns should be minimal, and there should not be any dead end aisles. Where conditions allow, space between facing rows of cars should contain grassy swales with indigenous vegetation. According to sustainable design principles, the parking spaces should slope towards the swales to allow drainage from the automobiles to be filtered and cleaned by the vegetation before the drainage water runs off the site.

Parking area design must also provide for pedestrian circulation—the movement of pedestrians to and from parked vehicles and the building entrance. This may be facilitated by the careful location of raised walks between aisles and striped crossings. Parking areas used at night must be well lit, generally one-half foot candle or more. To avoid the appearance of a sea of cars, carefully placed and designed landscape buffers may be used at the outer edges of parking areas. Curbed planters for trees and ground cover may be interspersed throughout paved parking areas to alleviate monotony.

Where justified by land costs, multilevel underground or above-ground parking structures may be economically feasible and preferable to surface parking. Such a determination can be made by considering the required area for parking and construction costs. For example, if land costs $30 per square foot, the cost to store a car at 400 square feet per vehicle is $12,000, to which must be added the cost of grading and paving. In order to park 300 vehicles on grade, 120,000 square feet of land, costing $3,600,000, is required. But suppose that parking structures cost $24 per square foot, and that 300 cars can be stored in three levels, 100 cars per level. Assuming the ground level costs $30 per square foot, to store 100 cars, and the two structured parking levels above cost $24 per square foot, the total cost to store 300 cars is $3,120,000 (40,000 SF × $30/SF + 2 × 40,000 SF × $24/SF = $3,120,000). In this case, the structured parking system is economically feasible.

PEDESTRIAN CIRCULATION

Pedestrian movement is an important though often neglected means of circulation. Central city enclaves, college campuses, and shopping centers all rely on pedestrian circulation. In developing site plans, careful provision must be made to allow pedestrians to move freely and easily. An understanding of the characteristics of movement and the physical dimensions of the body assists in the determination of the required widths of walkways, stairs, and entrances.

The area covered by a person, standing still, is approximately three square feet. This is based on a shoulder breadth of 24 inches and a body depth of 18 inches (an adult male). In order to stand comfortably in a crowd and move about easily without making body contact, a total of 13 square feet per person is required. A lesser area allowance for pedestrians tends to impede movement. If the allowable area is less than seven square feet per person, pedestrians tend to move as groups rather than as individuals. When each person occupies only three square feet or less, movement is extremely difficult and body contact may occur.

Walking involves balance, timing, and sight. It also requires spatial allowances for pacing, as well as sensing and reacting to other pedestrians. Movements on level surfaces are different from those on stairs or ramps.

Walkway capacities may be described in terms of both quality and rate of flow. At a rate of flow between one and two persons per minute, pedestrians can negotiate a two-foot wide strip of sidewalk unimpeded. Groups of pedestrians can be easily accommodated at that rate. The designer should be acquainted with the various walkway capacities. In general, sidewalks should be no less than five feet wide. Collector walkways, handling larger numbers of people, should be no less than six to ten feet in width.

These dimensions must be considered in conjunction with the circulation patterns and characteristics of the particular site. In shopping center malls, for instance, where a crisscrossing pattern occurs, additional space is needed. Because pedestrian movement follows the line of least resistance, it is quite common to see footpaths worn into the turf on college campuses. Paving such routes created by pedestrian usage is an old and practical technique.

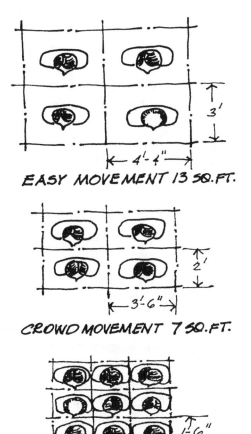

EASY MOVEMENT 13 SQ. FT.

CROWD MOVEMENT 7 SQ. FT.

NO MOVEMENT 3 SQ. FT.

PEDESTRIAN AREA ALLOWANCES

Figure 1.11

The pedestrian circulation system of a group of buildings or a single building should be clear and direct. A lack of clarity or an incoherent network will create considerable difficulty for the pedestrian. The most elaborate graphic signage system can only partly overcome the difficulties of a confusing walking pattern.

The primary objectives of good pedestrian circulation design are: safety, security, convenience, continuity, comfort, and attractiveness. To provide safety, pedestrian-vehicular separation is desirable. This can be achieved by grade-separated walkways above or below streets. Security can be achieved through clear sight lines and well lit pathways. Convenience requires the strategic location of walkways in relation to destinations. Vehicular traffic control systems can be placed and timed to assist pedestrian movement by controlling vehicles. Landscaping, paving, weather protection, fountains, benches, and other amenities can facilitate and enhance pedestrians' experiences in moving between spaces.

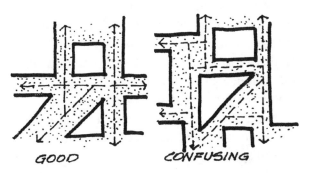

GOOD   CONFUSING

PEDESTRIAN CIRCULATION PATTERNS

Figure 1.12

PUBLIC TRANSIT

In the years following World War II, American cities experienced their greatest era of growth and expansion. This occurred at a time when more and more people were able to realize a long-held dream, to own an automobile.

At the same time our public transit systems, most of them developed 50 or more years earlier, were in a state of disrepair and neglect, many barely operating. The same was true of many old rail commuter systems.

After World War II, the federal government created a low-interest home mortgage financing program. In the 1950s, it initiated the interstate highway system. Together, these two programs were responsible for the creation of the post-war American suburb, shopping center, and industrial park.

However, no plan was established to rebuild, let alone enlarge, public urban transit systems. The fact is that both individual transportation and collective transportation are needed in order to have an efficient and livable metropolis. All urban transportation is public, to a great degree. Automobiles operate on public streets, as do buses. Most rail rapid transit systems and commuter systems are also publicly owned. The only portions of the automobile transit system that are not public are the automobile itself and the garage or parking space in which it is stored. Thus, the terms "individual" and "collective" transportation both refer to public systems, and should be considered as such when one examines the direct and indirect costs of both systems.

We have learned rather late that a metropolis needs both individual and collective transportation, and we are still struggling to achieve a balance. It is also true that neither system operates without public intervention: building and maintaining roadways; or building and maintaining buses, rail rapid transit systems, and commuter rail systems.

Transportation planning must be coupled with land use planning. When one knows where people are, and where they go, one can plan effective means for transporting them, by individual or collective means of transit. Here density plays an important role, for no collective transit system can be operated economically below an average population density of approximately 30 persons per acre. Such a threshold density is required to provide enough users going in the same direction at the same time to support collective transit. This density is perfectly livable, although it exceeds the

average of the typical American suburb, but not the overall metropolis. It also means a much more thoughtful and careful type of residential community design, such as a planned unit development (PUD), in which individual, row, walk-up, and elevator residences are sensitively grouped. To have effective collective transit systems it is necessary to coordinate outlying development with rail rapid transit systems and bus systems, which is occurring now. Had it occurred back in the 1950s, our cities would be considerably more livable and efficient.

An informed designer should know the rudiments of a collective transit system.

Walking is the most basic form of urban transportation, especially in high density areas. Walking speed varies from 2 1/2 to 4 1/2 miles per hour. The maximum distance that most people will walk to a destination is a quarter- to a half-mile.

The *local bus* is useful for trips in medium density areas, and for short trips in medium to high density areas. Buses travel at an average of 15 to 30 miles per hour. We are willing to spend up to a half-hour for most urban travel, whatever the mode.

The *express bus* is useful between medium density areas, within high density areas, and at specially planned and convenient terminals in high density areas. It travels at an average of 40 to 60 miles per hour.

Rail rapid transit, averaging 40 to 70 miles per hour, is useful between medium density areas, between high density areas, and for short trips within high density areas. It requires concentrations of people in time or in place to operate effectively.

One often hears of exotic transport devices which promise to solve the urban transportation problem. These include the "light rail" system, which is simply another name for the street car. Another is the so-called "monorail." Few monorail systems are true one-rail systems; most, in fact, have several rails. They have the serious limitation of being located only above ground, which may not be possible in some central city areas. A truly useful rail rapid transit system should be capable of being located above, below, or at ground level and thus fully adaptable, physically, to the area it serves. Sustainable design planning encourages TOD (Transit Oriented Design) development. If housing, commercial, and institutional development can be located near existing mass transit, then users of these developments will have more travel options— and not be totally dependent on the automobile. This approach saves energy and allows the buyers of the TOD property to spend less money on transit and more on their own properties.

A fully developed urban transportation system must include both individual and collective systems, and at the scale of today's regionalized metropolis. We have such a system for individual transit: the private automobile. We do not yet have such systems for collective transit. Fully developed, they would include walking, buses at various speeds, rail rapid transit (surface, underground, and elevated), commuter rail, and high-speed interurban rail systems, such as those in Europe and Japan.

PROVISIONS FOR THE HANDICAPPED

There are, at present, between 18 and 20 million people in the United States with physical handicaps. To accommodate them, special construction details are needed, particularly to facilitate their unimpeded movement. Impediments to such movement are referred to as "architectural barriers." In recent years, public interest in the accommodation of the handicapped has resulted in the passage of laws that assure that barriers are not present in public buildings and spaces. Designers should be familiar with the standards that have been developed to eliminate and avoid architectural barriers.

There are several types of disabilities, each requiring special consideration in planning and design. We have briefly mentioned handicapped parking requirements, and other aspects of design for the handicapped are discussed below. The following are brief descriptions of the various forms of handicaps:

Non-ambulatory disabilities confine persons to wheelchairs.

Semi-ambulatory disabilities cause persons to walk with insecurity or difficulty and may necessitate the use of crutches, walkers, or braces.

Coordination disabilities are manifested by impairments of muscle control to the limbs.

Sight disabilities affect sight totally or partially, to the extent that an individual functioning in public areas is insecure and prone to injury.

Hearing disabilities affect hearing ability totally or partially, to the extent that an individual functioning in public areas is insecure or prone to injury due to an inability to communicate, or to hear warning signals.

The non-ambulatory disabilities, which confine persons to wheelchairs, are of particular concern in design and planning, since they affect the physical layout and configuration of sites and buildings.

One should begin with an understanding of the basic characteristics of wheelchair usage. The basic manual wheelchair is shown in Figure 1.13. The electric wheelchair is similar, but about nine inches longer. The minimum space for turning 180 degrees is a clear space 60 inches in diameter.

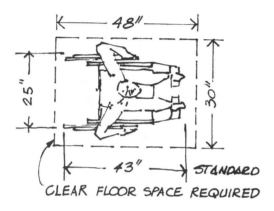

CLEAR FLOOR SPACE REQUIRED

BASIC WHEELCHAIR CRITERIA
Figure 1.13

The minimum width required for two wheelchairs to pass each other is 60 inches. This suggests that all public walks should be no less than five feet wide. Furthermore, walks should not have a gradient greater than 1:20 (5 percent) with a maximum cross gradient (slope) of 1:50 (2 percent). Where an accessible walk crosses a curb, the width of the walk should be three feet minimum plus flared sides that slope a maximum of 1:10. For example, where the curb height of a walk is six inches, a minimum curb cutout of 13 feet in length is necessary.

Such walks should have continuing common surfaces, without abrupt changes of slope. Nor should they be interrupted by cracks or breaks creating edges of one-half inch or more in height. Wherever walks join other walks, driveways, or curbs, they should blend to a common

level. The pitch of such surface blends should not exceed a gradient of 1:12 (8 1/3 percent).

A curb ramp is preferably constructed by cutting into a curb and grading a section of walk, creating an inclined section as shown in the sketches on the following page. Alternatively, the level of the lower pavement may be built up, as shown. Regardless of its configuration, the incline of a curb ramp should not exceed 1:12 (8 1/3 percent).

Curb cutouts should be identified by a 1/16 inch yellow abrasive anti-slip epoxy finish applied to the entire area of the curb cutout, or by abrasive strips 1/16 inch thick and two to three inches wide. These should be applied across each curb cutout surface at intervals of three inches. The cutout areas of curb cutouts, traffic island passageways, and the curb edging (for at least three feet on each side of a curb cutout) should be painted yellow. Where traffic islands interrupt pedestrian crossings, a cutout area at paved area level not less than three feet in width should be provided.

Ramps should be employed wherever a vertical drop is greater than one-half inch. The gradient should not exceed 1:12 (8 1/3 percent) and preferably be 1:16 (6 1/4 percent) whenever possible. Ramps should be a minimum of three feet wide and not exceed 30 feet in length. At each end of each inclined section, and at each turning point, a level area at least five feet long should be provided. Handrails should be located at each side of a ramp if its rise is greater than 6 inches or its run is greater than 72 inches. A protective curb should be installed on the side where a ramp is above finish grade.

Parking spaces for the handicapped require special design and dimensions. They should always be located along the shortest possible circulation route to an accessible building entrance. The spaces should be a minimum of eight feet wide with a five-foot wide access aisle between every two spaces. The access aisles should, in turn, be directly connected to accessible walks. The designated spaces should be as close as possible, but never more than 200 feet from a building's entrance, and they should be clearly designated by an unobstructed sign showing the symbol of accessibility.

The number of spaces set aside for handicapped persons depends on the use of the facility. In parking areas concerned with academic or administrative functions the suggested ratios are as follows:

Capacity of Parking Lot	Number of Handicapped Spaces
7–50	2 minimum
51–100	3 minimum
101–150	5 minimum
over 150	5 plus 2 minimum for every additional 100

Areas designated for handicapped parking should be properly illuminated for after-dark usage.

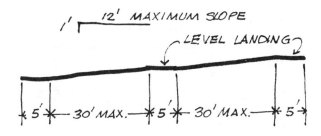

RAMP DESIGN CRITERIA
Figure 1.14

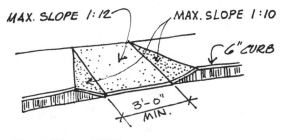

FLARED SIDES

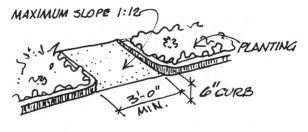

RETURNED CURB

BUILT-UP

PARALLEL

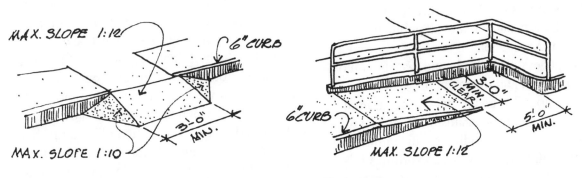

TYPICAL CURB RAMPS
Figure 1.15

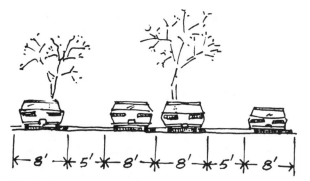

PARKING FOR THE HANDICAPPED
Figure 1.16

Other design criteria for accommodating the handicapped include the design of doors, door hardware, stairs, elevators, restrooms, drinking fountains, telephones, signage, and vending machines. Also included are such special-use facilities as those for performing arts, school laboratories, and kitchens.

SERVICES AND UTILITIES

The development of land for residential, commercial, industrial and community uses depends, to a large extent, on the availability of various services and utilities. These include water, gas, electricity, communication systems, wastewater systems, drainage systems, and flood control. Consideration must also be given to methods of trash collection, fire protection, mail distribution, snow removal, public transportation, and provision for public health and safety. In general, the supply and distribution of water, collection and treatment of wastewater, collection, storage, and ultimate disposition of storm water, protection against damage due to flooding, as well as providing for the public's health and safety, are services and utilities furnished by public agencies. Telephone service is always provided by private companies, while electricity, gas, and transportation services are provided by either privately-owned util-

ity companies or public agencies, depending on the community. Privately owned utilities operate under a franchise and are regulated by a governmental agency, such as a state utilities commission.

Sustainable design planning encourages "infill" development. This is development that fills in between existing buildings. This approach has the following advantages:

- Possible lower first cost (reusing existing infrastructure rather than creating new systems)

- Less environmental impact (not disturbing an existing, undisturbed, natural open space)

- Creating higher density development, which more efficiently uses the infrastructure and supports nearby public transit, parks, and commercial districts

The means of distribution are as varied as the nature of the services and utilities themselves. Some are transported in conduits, pipes, channels, tunnels, or ditches. Others depend on cables or wires for distribution. The space beneath the public street right-of-way is the most logical and efficient location for services to buildings. These may include wastewater lines, water mains, gas mains, electric power conduits, cable television lines, and steam lines. Of course, all of these must be connected to the buildings they service. Planning for underground utility installations in a street right-of-way is the responsibility of the local government, which has jurisdiction over the streets. Although cooperation of all utilities is essential, local government must exercise authority to determine locations, should conflicts occur.

In developing plans for underground utility locations, the following general principles should be observed:

1. Wastewater lines, because of their gravity flow requirements, should have first priority.

2. Trunk (main) lines should not be located in major traffic arteries, if possible.

3. Trunk lines for several utilities should not be located in the same street.

4. The center of the street should be reserved for the wastewater lines, unless the street is sufficiently wide to accommodate a dual wastewater system (separate waste lines for each side).

5. All utility installations required for the next five years should be installed before a street is paved. This includes the service lines to the curb or property line.

Power lines are generally located above ground, where even the most carefully designed landscaping cannot conceal them. However, as a result of public pressure, more and more such lines are being placed underground, when it can be justified economically.

Water Supply and Distribution

Water is essential to the life and well-being of a community. Its economical supply and distribution is a major element in a community's comprehensive development plan. Water availability plays an important role in determining the location, patterns of growth, and prosperity of cities. Water is required for human consumption, washing, fire fighting, street cleaning, landscape irrigation, air conditioning, manufacturing, and recreation. Future demands in urban areas are based on population projections. Experience indicates an average demand of 150 gallons of water per capita per day. However, demands vary from community to community depending on a variety of factors, such as the

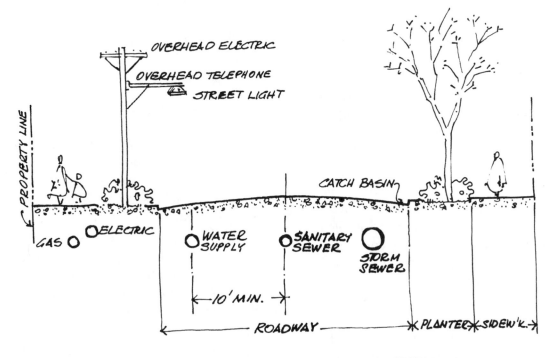

GENERAL LOCATION OF UTILITIES
Figure 1.17

amount and types of industry, climate, open space and cost.

A water supply system consists of components that procure, treat, and distribute water to users. It includes these principal features:

1. Sources, which include lakes, rivers, streams, and wells which tap underground water. (Desalination projects in coastal areas may become a future source of water supply.)
2. Transmission mains, including aqueducts, canals, and pipelines, which transmit raw water to treatment plants or to the distribution systems of untreated water.
3. Water treatment plants.
4. Distribution systems, which convey treated water to the users' properties. The systems may include reservoirs and pumping stations.
5. Metered connections between the distribution system and users' properties.

The type of water supply distribution network in an urban area is determined by the street plan, urban density, and topography. Water supply systems are installed in either a branch pattern or a gridiron pattern. Gridiron patterns can be improved by installing "loop header" systems in high density urban areas, thereby ensuring supply from more than one direction.

In densely populated areas, the single or dual main grid system is prevalent. Dual main systems (i.e., mains and service headers located on both sides of streets) are more common because they reduce the length and cost of service runs to properties.

Conduit and piping used in distribution system mains may be cast iron, wrought iron, steel, or plastic. Where larger sizes are required, they may be reinforced concrete.

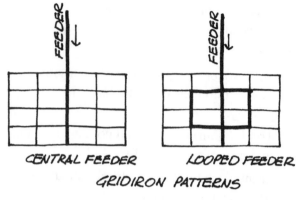

CENTRAL FEEDER   LOOPED FEEDER
GRIDIRON PATTERNS

WATER SUPPLY SYSTEMS
Figure 1.18

Water main sizes, most often determined by fire protection requirements, are generally 6″ in typical residential areas and 8″ in high density districts. Water meters and shut-off valves are usually located at the user's property line. Main line valves are located so that no single break will affect more than approximately 500 feet of water main. Fire hydrants are usually spaced 150 feet apart in high density districts and about 600 feet apart in suburban areas.

Public water supply is not usually justified in areas where the population density is less than 1,000 persons per square mile.

Wastewater Systems

The collection and treatment of wastewater are fundamental considerations in planning urban developments. A wastewater system's function is to collect and dispose of sanitary wastes from plumbing fixtures and other similar collection points. The liquid wastes are conveyed to a point of disposal, where they are treated before being discharged into a body of water, or otherwise disposed of. Local water quality standards determine the extent of treatment required.

The design of wastewater systems involves population projections, industrial growth, topography, soil conditions, rainfall, water quality standards, and water reclamation. Since wastewater lines flow by gravity, they follow the direction of the natural surface drainage system. Consequently, these systems may cross political boundaries. As a result, many urbanized areas have created sanitary districts, which are special governmental units which have administrative control of the wastewater system.

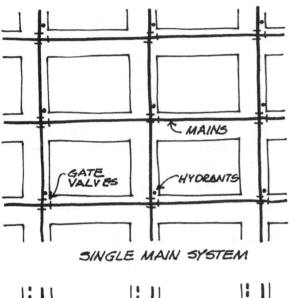

SINGLE MAIN SYSTEM

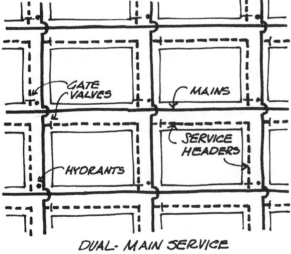

DUAL-MAIN SERVICE

GRID DISTRIBUTION SYSTEMS

Figure 1.19

Wastewater collection systems in urban areas are arranged in networks, allowing gravity flow to treatment or disposal points. Waste-

water lines are maintained at a constant slope, depending on the size of lines and capacity of flow. The grades are sufficient to provide velocities (no less than 2 1/2 feet per second and no more than 10 feet per second) to convey solid materials.

Grades required to transport solids range form one-half to two percent. "Drop manholes" or pump lift stations are located wherever topographic conditions require. Where waste is pumped over extensive horizontal distances the conduit is termed a "force main."

Although collection networks must be adapted to topography, grid patterns established by street layouts dictate, to a large extent, the location of wastewater lines. Grade requirements and relationships to adjacent building foundations or basements result in considerable variation in the depth of wastewater lines below ground level. This generally results in wastewater mains being the lowest structures below street level. The wastewater main is usually a single line at the center of the street, although in high density districts, there may be two lines, one on each side of the street. Connections to buildings must also be sloped although, if unavoidable, they may also be pumped. Materials used for wastewater conduits include vitrified clay, cast iron, and more recently, plastic and lightweight fiberglass-reinforced mortar plastic. Diameters are up to 4 feet and length up to 20 feet.

Wastewater may contain materials which are hazardous to health and thus unsuitable for human, industrial, or commercial uses, even after treatment. Treatment plants must be adequately sized to be compatible in capacity and function with the collection system. Proper treatment involves large plants staffed by technically competent personnel.

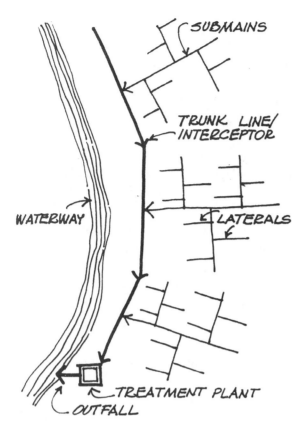

SUBMAINS

TRUNK LINE/
INTERCEPTOR

WATERWAY

LATERALS

TREATMENT PLANT

OUTFALL

TYPICAL WASTEWATER SYSTEM
Figure 1.20

Electrical Utility Facilities

Modern urban areas cannot function without electricity. This vital utility is a necessity for every home, office building, and factory. Frequently, urban transportation also depends on it. Electrical power is generated primarily by turbines powered by steam produced by burning coal, oil, or gas, or sometimes by water power. Some power plants utilize nuclear reactors to produce the heat to transform water to steam. Power plants are generally large facilities, supplying power to more than one community. Smaller plants that use diesel-driven generators are commonly found in small communities. Hydroelectric plants must, obviously, be located adjacent to water. Nuclear plants are away from urban centers.

The transmission and distribution of power poses special problems. In the past, electricity brought to each user was carried by overhead wires supported by power poles or transmission towers. These were located along streets and alleys, or along rights-of-way at the rear of properties. Aesthetic considerations and technical advances have made it possible to locate electric distribution lines underground. An underground distribution system must be coordinated with street improvement plans. Substations are located so as to form "service areas." Substations may be located underground, in buildings, or in enclosures screened by walls, fences, or landscaping.

Street lighting contributes to vehicular and pedestrian safety. Consideration should be given to the appearance of lighting poles and fixtures. Their height and spacing should be such as to achieve a uniform light pattern.

Telephone and Telegraph

Telephone and telegraph utilities provide communication links essential to urban areas. This involves the proper placement and location of telephone lines and exchanges. Telephone trunk lines are generally placed in underground conduits in street rights-of-way. Local lines may, however, be placed on poles, generally shared with power lines.

Fire and police alarm systems are closely related to telephone systems. Continuity in service is of major importance in emergency and disaster situations. Wires from alarm or call boxes are generally placed in underground conduit.

CATV

Cable antenna television is popular in urban areas that lack conventional TV broadcast facilities, or where building heights, topographical features, mineral deposits and other conditions make conventional reception unsatisfactory. In addition, cable television often provides additional channels for viewing, which are unavailable with conventional reception. A CATV system consists of a central station where signals are received on a community antenna and transmitted over a network of coaxial cable. The cable is generally attached to electric power, telephone, or joint-use poles located above the ground. Or, it may be buried along with electric and telephone systems, sometimes in a common trench.

Gas Utility Systems

Gas is one of the most useful fuels for home and industry. Most gas is natural gas, which is carried over long distances in pressurized transmission pipes. These may be located within the street right-of-way, usually in the sidewalk area on both sides of the street, or in alleys or rear lot easements. Regulating stations are located in various parts of a community. In residential areas, they are most often placed in an underground vault. Where natural gas is not available, gas may be manufactured. Such manufacturing facilities, along with storage tanks, are located in industrial areas.

Gas distribution networks are similar in layout to water supply systems, including branching and looped patterns. As in water systems, loops provide alternate directions of supply in case of failures. The primary pipe material is welded steel, although some older systems employ cast iron pipes, since these were the first to be used by the gas industry. A primary problem associated with the use of steel in direct burial systems is corrosion. Asphalt, coal, tar, and extruded and taped plastic compounds are used to control corrosion. Auxiliary equipment in distribution systems includes valves, pressure regulating stations, flow meters and, in some instances, compressor stations.

Flood Control and Drainage Systems

When an urban area is developed, paving and roofs replace absorbent soil and vegetation, reducing the ability of the area to contain storm water. The rush of surface water from a storm can thus cause severe flooding, or it can overload streams and rivers that, in turn, also results in flooding. Consequently, urban planning must consider the disposition of surface water runoff in newly developed areas and flood protection for existing developments.

Sustainable design planning encourages the architect to avoid building in the floodplain—especially below the 100-year flood elevation.

"Storm water" refers to the flow of water on ground surfaces or drainage channels produced by rainfall or melting snow. It must be collected, stored, and conducted to its eventual outlet so as to avoid water damage. The amount of storm water to be managed depends upon the size, shape, and topography of the watershed, the amount of rainfall or snow accumulation, ground surface conditions (wooded areas, turfed areas, bare ground, paved areas, or buildings), and soil characteristics. Since watersheds and streams do not correspond to municipal boundaries, planning for storm water systems must be done regionally. This is a twofold process: the first deals with the pattern of land usage and the consequent effects on surface conditions, and the second involves the urban drainage system.

The management of surface drainage may involve regulation of density, minimizing paved surfaces, maximizing planted areas, careful grading to ensure gentle slopes and positive flow, and utilizing ditches, check dams, and culverts. However, where roof and paved areas increase runoff, drainage structures are needed to prevent flooding.

A storm drainage system consists of the drainage surface, open gutters and ditches, and underground pipes, usually made of vitrified clay connected by manholes and fed by inlets. Drainage pipes larger than 42 inches in diameter are made of concrete. Modern storm drainage systems are entirely separate from wastewater systems to minimize the volume that must be handled in wastewater treatment plants, and to prevent the overloading of sanitary waste conduits.

The drainage of an area is affected by the ground across which the surface water flows. As the quantity of water increases, it develops it own path, eventually leading to open street gutters. Once in the street, the water may be allowed to flow for some distance before being collected and conducted in underground drains. Since water should be prevented from flowing across streets or walks, it should be collected at least once at the lowest corner of a typical city block.

Water may travel 1,000 feet before reaching a collection point for a storm sewer, but should avoid turning sharp corners or meeting sudden obstructions to flow. Metal gratings are set in gutters or curb faces at inlets to prevent debris from entering the system. From these inlets, water is conducted by short branch lines to the main storm drain. These junctions are generally located at manholes that are spaced about 500 feet apart. Manholes are also located at the ends of lines and at each change in direction. Drainage lines are generally designed with sufficient slope so that the velocity of flow will promote self-cleaning. This may be assumed to be 0.3 percent minimum, which develops a flow speed of about two feet per second. Slopes resulting in velocities exceeding 10 per second should be avoided.

A storm drainage system is generally laid out in plan and elevation from the point of discharge. The lines are designed to minimize length of runs and number of manholes. Profiles are plotted and pipe sizes computed, the latter based on varied criteria of rainfall, runoff, drainage, flow velocity, and properties of the pipe. Storm sewers are most often located within the street right-of-way. In some instances, however, it is necessary to obtain easements for these facilities through private property.

SUMMARY

Although circulation systems, as such, are not part of architectural design, it is necessary for architects to have an understanding of such systems, since they influence how a building is sited, particularly its entrance points. These circulation systems include those for vehicles and pedestrians, as well as public transit systems.

Parking, obviously, also has great influence on building design, particularly when incorporated into a building.

Provisions to make buildings and facilities accessible and usable by the handicapped are generally required, and the necessary elements should be carefully integrated into the design.

Utility systems, while largely unseen, must also be understood, since they affect land and site planning.

Last but far from least, surface water management and site topography are important aspects of all building design.

LESSON 1 QUIZ

1. What type of circulation system responds most sympathetically to the existing natural environment?

   A. Grid system

   B. Linear system

   C. Curvilinear system

   D. Radial system

2. To move large volumes of traffic at high speed, the most effective type of circulation system is

   A. highways.   C. arterials.

   B. expressways.   D. distributors.

3. Land use development patterns are most frequently determined by

   A. topographic factors.

   B. climatic factors.

   C. utility systems.

   D. street systems.

4. The primary advantage of 60-degree parking is that it

   A. saves space.

   B. is easier to use.

   C. is safer to use.

   D. costs less to construct.

5. A neighborhood shopping center is best located at

   A. the intersection of an arterial and collector street.

   B. the intersection of two local streets.

   C. the foot of an expressway ramp.

   D. the interchange of an expressway.

6. From among the following street design criteria, select those that are correct.

   I.   Curb radii should be 12 feet minimum.

   II. Compound curves are preferred over simple curves.

   III. Traffic lanes should be about 12 feet wide.

   IV. Parking lanes should generally be avoided.

   V.   Intersections should be at right angles wherever possible.

   A. I and IV   C. II, III, and IV

   B. I, III, and V   D. I, III, IV, and V

7. Power lines are generally located above, rather than below, ground because they are

   A. easier to repair.

   B. faster to install.

   C. less costly.

   D. less dangerous.

8. From among the following handicapped design criteria, select the INCORRECT statement.

   A. Wheelchair paths should not exceed a 1:20 grade.

   B. Wheelchair ramps should not exceed a 1:12 grade.

   C. Wheelchair ramps should not exceed 30 feet in length.

   D. Wheelchair turning spaces should not be less than three feet square.

9. Which of the following should be avoided in the design of a large parking lot?

   I.   Acute angle parking

   II. Ramped exit driveway

   III. Dead level paved areas

   IV. Dead end aisles

   V. Pedestrian circulation

A. III and IV

B. III and V

C. I, II, and V

D. II, III, and IV

10. The primary objective of good pedestrian circulation is

A. economy.

B. permanence.

C. safety.

D. speed.

SITE ASSESSMENT AND SITE WORK

INTRODUCTION

A building project generally begins with the selection of a particular site. The exact location of the site, as well as its orientation, topography, existing vegetation, and subsoil conditions, all influence the design of the building, including the materials and methods of construction. In some cases, the client may contact the architect with property deed and survey in one hand and the building program in the other hand. At other times, however, the architect may be approached with several alternative sites, each of which satisfies the specific program. In those cases, the architect must examine the choices in

order to recommend the site that will best meet the program's requirements.

In order for the architect to make this professional judgment, all potential sites should be verified for satisfactory size, topography, orientation, and access, and the availability of utilities, such as water, electricity, and gas. In addition, the site must be checked for all restrictions imposed by city, state, and federal regulations, such as zoning, easements, and subsurface rights. A final and perhaps most important criterion: one must verify that the soil is adequate to support the intended structure.

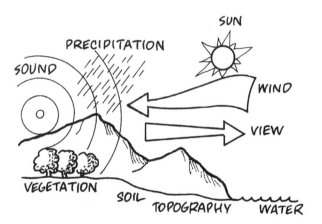

SITE CONSIDERATIONS
Figure 2.1

The geographical location of the site is most often established by the client. Thus, climatic factors, such as sun, wind, precipitation, and temperature, are matters of fact rather than choice. However, the architect may consider such variables as topography, vegetation, sound, and orientation relative to sun and views. The land forms and ground slopes affect a building's foundation, drainage, and microclimate. Vegetation, too, affects the site's microclimate, as well as its views, solar radiation, and sound travel. Prevailing exterior sounds affect the orientation of the building mass, the choice of materials, and sound control methods employed. Finally, orientation affects solar radiation, natural ventilation, potential views, and ease of access to the site.

CLIMATE

General

The climate of an area is described in quantitative data, which include the range and distribution of temperatures, the hours of sunshine, the direction and velocity of winds, precipitation, and humidity. A region's climate is modified by local conditions, which include the effects of topography, structures, exposure, ground cover, elevation, and water bodies. Such local variation in climate is known as the *microclimate*.

People are comfortable within a narrow range of related conditions, including temperature, humidity, air movement, and air quality. This is known as the *comfort zone*, and although it varies slightly from one individual to another, the temperature generally ranges from 65° to 75°F, with 30 to 60 percent relative humidity. At higher temperatures, air movement or mechanical cooling is necessary to maintain comfort, while at lower temperatures heating must be provided in order to maintain comfort. At excessively low humidities, moisture must be added to the air, and at excessively high humidities, moisture must be removed in order to maintain comfort.

The architect, with the help of a mechanical engineer, has the responsibility of designing for indoor climatic comfort. It is possible to alleviate the extremes of climate, both indoors and out, through judicious planning, considering the orientation of the building, the building's fenestration and materials, ground cover and planting, and shading or exposure to sun. Sustainable design encourages a holistic approach that allows the architect to understand all the

environmental issues (climate, sunlight, soil conditions, etc.) and infrastructure components (mass transit, roads, utilities, etc.) before initiating the design process.

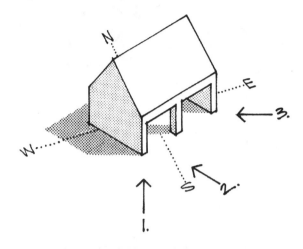

1. EVENING SUN BLOCKED
2. MID-DAY SUN CAN ENTER IN WINTER - BUT MAY BE BLOCKED OUT IN SUMMER
3. MORNING SUN ENTERS

Figure 2.2

Orientation

The ideal orientation for a structure in the northern hemisphere is slightly east of south, since the south side of a building receives more radiation in winter and less in summer. With the major glass areas of a building facing south, the benefit of winter sunlight to the interior of a building is most fully realized. The east and west sides receive low morning and late afternoon sun in summer. Since it is difficult to shade windows against direct sunlight on these sides, fenestration should be kept to a minimum in order to avoid excessive heat gain in summer. Large glass areas on the west side of a building have an additional problem if the west side faces a highly reflective surface, such as a body of water. The north side of a building receives little sun radiation, summer or winter. An advantage of north light, however, is its

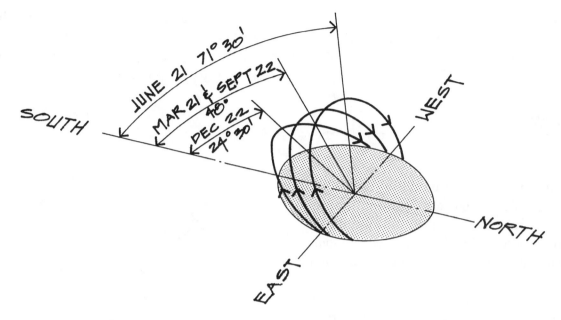

THE SUN'S PATH AT 42° NORTH LATITUDE

Figure 2.3

relatively even intensity, making it ideal for such uses as an artist's studio or an architect's drafting room.

There are, of course, many factors other than climate that must be considered before the orientation and fenestration of a building are determined. The existing street pattern, the

orientation of neighboring structures, and aesthetic compatibility must also be taken into account.

The Sun's Path

Knowledge of the sun's movement is necessary to design properly for sun control. The sun rises in the east and sets in the west, and in the

CITY	NORTH LATITUDE	JUNE 21	MARCH 21 & SEPT 22	DEC 22
SEATTLE	47°30'	66°	42°30'	19°
MINNEAPOLIS	45°	68°30'	45°	21°30'
CHICAGO	42°	71°30'	48°	24°30'
NEW YORK	40°45'	72°43'	49°15'	25°45'
LOS ANGELES	34°	79°30'	56°	32°30'
MIAMI	25°45'	87'45'	64°15'	40°45'

NOON SOLAR ANGLE

Figure 2.4

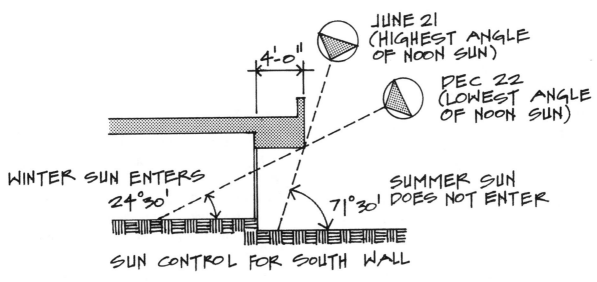

Figure 2.5

northern hemisphere, the sun's path is inclined southerly. The angle that the noon sun makes with the horizon is maximum at the summer solstice, June 21, and minimum at the winter solstice, December 22. The angle is halfway between these extremes at both the vernal equinox, March 21, and autumnal equinox, September 22. The angles in the diagram in Figure 2.3 apply to areas located at 42° north latitude, such as Chicago. In higher (more northerly) latitudes, such as Seattle, the sun's angle with the horizon (altitude) is smaller all year round. In lower (more southerly) latitudes, such as Los Angeles, the sun's altitude is higher all year round. As a result, heat transmission through walls is more important in the high (northerly) latitudes, while heat transmission through roofs is more important in the low (southerly) latitudes. Solar angles for a few selected cities are shown in Figure 2.4.

Sun Control

The sun control provided by a four-foot roof overhang over the south wall at 42° north latitude is illustrated in Figure 2.5.

In more southerly latitudes, the same amount of sun control can be obtained with a shorter overhang, while in more northerly latitudes, a longer overhang is needed to compensate for the lower sun angle.

Sun controls in the form of overhangs, fins, or louvers are widely used to limit the amount of solar energy entering a building in summer months. Sun shields may be an integral part of the building, such as a cantilevered floor or roof overhang, or they may be a device attached to the structure. They may be fixed or adjustable, they may emphasize vertical or horizontal elements, or they may form a grid pattern. Whatever their design, they should admit light and view, exclude the sun's heat and glare during the warmer months, but admit solar heat during the winter. The use of sun shields outside of a building is far more effective than trying to reflect or absorb the heat after it contacts the building surface.

Properly designed sun shading devices can reduce heat gain substantially—enough to lower the cost of air conditioning installation and operation by 15 percent or more. However, sun shields have a significant initial cost, require regular maintenance, and must be designed to minimize the loss of natural light in the building.

In the northern hemisphere, horizontal overhangs are effective for southern exposures, while vertical fins are effective for east and west exposures. Vertical baffles parallel to and outside building walls are effective for all exposures. If exterior sun controls cannot be used, interior devices such as shades or blinds may be necessary, but they are not nearly as effective as exterior devices.

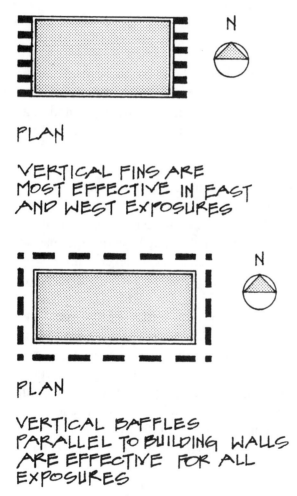

PLAN

VERTICAL FINS ARE MOST EFFECTIVE IN EAST AND WEST EXPOSURES

PLAN

VERTICAL BAFFLES PARALLEL TO BUILDING WALLS ARE EFFECTIVE FOR ALL EXPOSURES

Figure 2.6

Low buildings may be effectively shaded by deciduous trees, which block the summer sun while permitting the winter sun to enter. Trees may also be placed to intercept winter winds,

while allowing cooling summer breezes to pass. Trees also reduce noise, filter air, reduce glare, provide a feeling of privacy and protection, and are an aesthetic asset.

Winds

Wind intensities and directions vary widely in different parts of the country. Data collected over the past 50 years has been used as the basis of a wind speed map, as well as a table of wind pressures. The map in Figure 2.7, which is reproduced from the Uniform Building Code, indicates that most areas have a basic wind speed of 70 to 80 miles per hour. This corresponds to a pressure of 13 to 17 pounds per square foot at a height of 30 feet, as shown in UBC Table No. 23-F, reproduced in Table 2.1.

Higher wind speeds occur on the Gulf Coast from Florida to Texas, and on the Atlantic Coast, where buildings must incorporate structural systems that are designed to resist very high wind forces.

Wind loads increase with height, while at ground level, wind loads decrease to almost zero. The shape and orientation of a structure also affect wind load pressures.

Wind pressure is expressed in pounds per square foot (psf), and varies as the square of the wind velocity in miles per hour (mph). Thus, a wind velocity of 70 mph causes a wind pressure of about 13 psf. If the wind velocity doubles, the wind pressure increases fourfold, to about 50 psf.

The walls of a building must be designed to withstand wind loads, as well as prevent undesirable wind infiltration into the building. The building's supporting structure must be designed to resist wind loads, and for that reason the structural system of a tall building in a high wind area, such as the Gulf Coast, is likely

TABLE NO. 23-F—WIND STAGNATION PRESSURE (q_s) AT STANDARD HEIGHT OF 30 FEET							
Basic wind speed (mph)[1]	70	80	90	100	110	120	130
Pressure q_s (psf)	13	17	21	26	31	37	44
[1] Wind speed from Section 2311 (b).							

Table 2.1

to be considerably more expensive than for the same building in an area with lower wind loads.

In evaluating the effects of wind on a building, modifications to the wind pattern caused by local topography and structures should be studied. Wind direction and intensity must also be considered in relation to climate, and the effect it may have on a building's heating or cooling. Distinction should be made between winter winds, which should be blocked as much as possible, and cooling summer winds, which should be admitted and utilized as much as possible.

Windbreaks can be used to block undesirable winds. Wind tunnel experiments have shown that tree windbreaks are particularly effective in protecting large downwind areas. Protection from winter wind improves outdoor comfort

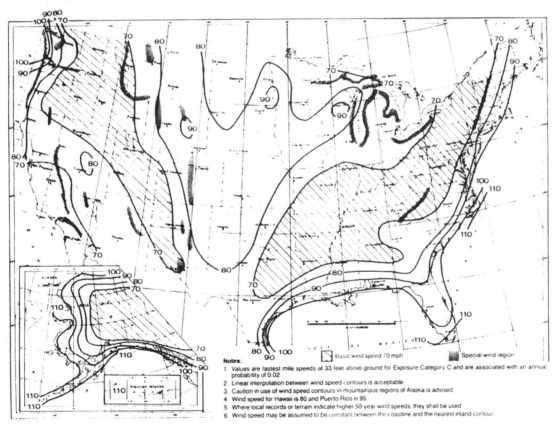

BASIC WIND SPEEDS IN MILES PER HOUR

Figure 2.7

conditions, as well as reducing the heating requirements for buildings so protected.

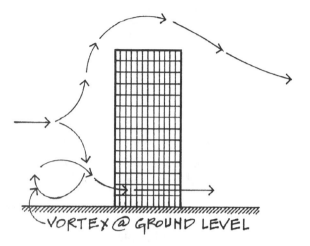

VORTEX @ GROUND LEVEL

WIND PATTERNS ON TALL BUILDINGS

Figure 2.8

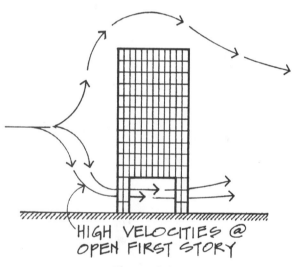

HIGH VELOCITIES @ OPEN FIRST STORY

Figure 2.9

With the increase in the number of high-rise buildings has come an increased awareness of the effects of winds on buildings, as well as the effects of buildings on wind patterns. Tall buildings act as windbreaks. Part of the wind blows up and over the roof, and part flows down the face of the building, creating a vortex of high velocity near the ground. Open plazas at the ground level of large buildings, while aesthetically desirable, may be uncomfortably

windy at certain times. A similar effect occurs when the ground level of a building is open. The open area acts as a wind tunnel, and wind velocities may be considerably increased.

There are no simple solutions to these problems. Air movement data for urban areas must be researched, studied, and integrated with other environmental influences. Proper urban design could induce the flow of cooling air masses into cities in summer, while blocking cold winds in winter.

Fenestration

Windows allow people to look out from a building, in addition to admitting light, air (if they are openable), and solar radiation. Light and view are vital to psychological well being. Most building inhabitants, when given the choice, express a preference for openable windows. The sustainable design approach has taught us that occupants need better control of their internal environment than formerly believed. Engineers and architects are increasingly exploring the option of operable windows, even in high-rise construction.

Glass allows solar energy to enter the building, and this energy can be a useful source of natural heating during the colder months. But glass has a high initial cost, high maintenance, and rapid heat loss, up to 20 times greater than an insulated wall. The glass area of a building is one of the most critical elements as far as heat gain and heat loss are concerned. The disadvantages of glass can be partially overcome by the use of multiple glazing, heat absorbing or reflecting glass, sun control devices, or the use of smaller window openings.

Large glass areas, if properly shaded against direct sunlight, can reduce summer season cooling loads. Abundant daylight reduces electric lighting requirements, and this in turn reduces the heat generated by lighting. Daylighting, a technique used in the sustainable design approach, combines natural sunlight with dimmed overhead lighting to reduce energy costs and indoor lighting heat loads.

Exterior Materials

In order to reduce heat gain in summer and heat loss in winter, the roof and walls of buildings must be insulated. The measure of heat transmission is referred to as the *U-factor*, which is the number of BTU per hour that pass through one square foot of wall or roof when the difference between inside and outside air temperature is 1°F, with a steady rate of heat flow. The U value can vary widely, from as low as 0.064 for an insulated brick and plaster wall to over 1.0 for a single pane of ordinary glass. A low U value indicates slow heat loss or gain, while a high U value indicates rapid loss or gain of heat.

A significant factor in temperature control is the ability of a material to store heat. This is referred to as *thermal inertia*. Heavy materials absorb and store peak heat loads and later release them when the outside temperature drops. In areas with high diurnal (daily) temperature variation, concrete or masonry walls, which have high heat-storage capabilities, are used to store daytime heat and release it during the night, resulting in more balanced conditions. This situation is prevalent in hot, arid zones, such as Phoenix.

Semitropical areas, such as Miami, have little daily temperature variation, and the utilization of natural breezes with sun shading is quite effective there. If mechanical air cooling is used, shading and insulation are also helpful. Temperate areas, such as New York, should have heavy materials on the west wall to delay the impact of the late afternoon heat, and adequate insulation on all other walls. Cool areas,

such as Minneapolis, require materials similar to those of temperate areas, but with higher insulation values. Rigid insulation should be used at edges of slabs on grade to prevent heat loss in cool and temperate areas. Uninsulated slabs, however, are often satisfactory in warmer areas.

Climate causes the deterioration of materials in a variety of ways, primarily through the action of rain, humidity, frost, and sun. Metal corrodes near the ocean, and therefore, its use should be minimized, unless the required protective maintenance can be assured. In extremely dry areas, such as Palm Springs, California, and Tucson, Arizona, exposed wood tends to split and check. Hot, humid areas, on the other hand, are subject to mold and fungi, to which wood is particularly vulnerable.

Solar Heating and Cooling

In recent years the potential for energy shortages has stimulated the investigation of alternative energy sources. Among the realistic possibilities is the solar heating and, possibly, cooling of buildings. A number of buildings utilizing solar heating have been built, and the National Science Foundation estimates that by the year 2020, one third of all buildings will use some solar heating and cooling system. Heating buildings with solar energy is technically feasible, and it often compares favorably with existing conventional methods for cost effectiveness. Cooling with solar energy, however, is far more difficult. No complete solar heating and cooling system has yet been built and operated economically, but indications are that such systems may become feasible in the future.

If fossil fuels become more scarce and expensive, which is likely in the long run, solar energy will become a more attractive source for the heating, cooling, and electrical power needs of buildings. Sustainable design encourages architects to explore innovative technologies such as: solar hot water heating; PV (photovoltaic) paneling for electrical production; active and passive solar design for heating and cooling; fuel cells for electrical production; and ice storage systems for "off-peak" cooling. These technologies are currently in use in many parts of the world and the United States. Architects should investigate the innovative systems that are most appropriate for their climates.

Mechanical Equipment

While the details of mechanical equipment for heating and cooling of buildings is not the subject of this guide, some general observations should be made.

A critical design consideration for buildings in cool and temperate areas is the heating required during the colder part of the year. Even though one designs for maximum heat gain and minimum heat loss in winter, and some heating can be provided by natural solar radiation, most heat must be provided through mechanical means. The cost of heating is related to the difference between the outdoor winter design temperature and the indoor design temperature. The outdoor design temperature is about 0°F in Boston, 20°F in Los Angeles, and 40°F in Miami. The design temperature, incidentally, is a working average, and not the lowest temperature ever recorded in an area.

Desirable indoor temperatures vary with human activities. An example of a space with a desirable low indoor temperature is a gymnasium, while a high indoor temperature is desirable in a hospital room, where a patient's physical activity is minimal. Desirable indoor temperatures also vary with the season, being higher in the summer than in winter.

Hot, humid areas do not generally require any heating; however, cooling and dehumidifying the air and reducing heat gain are of prime importance.

Structures in hot, arid areas require both heating and cooling, the cooling being more critical. Buildings in the temperate zone also require both heating and cooling, while those in cool zones have a heavy heating demand and minimal cooling requirements.

Mechanical cooling systems are designed to provide an inside design temperature of about 75°F, when the outside design temperature varies from 90° to 110°F. Boston's outside design temperature is 85°F, while that of El Centro, California, is 110°F.

WATER

Introduction

Water is essential to all life. Yet in most parts of the United States and other highly developed countries, it is taken for granted, like the air we breathe. We turn on the faucet and it gushes forth; we clean, cook, bathe, flush, and irrigate with it, with little or no thought given to its source or continued availability.

But water is more than a physical necessity— it is a vital part of the landscape both aesthetically and emotionally. Since time immemorial, water has had a tremendous appeal for people. Whatever its form—pool, river, fountain, or waterfall—water is one of the most fascinating of all natural design elements.

Uses of Water

Water has many functions in site design. Some are aesthetic in nature—the still water of a lake is soothing and evokes a feeling of serenity.

However, the water body need not be natural to have a strong impact; the rigid geometry of a reflecting pool may also provide a contemplative setting. In contrast to the tranquility of still water, the swift moving water of a fountain or waterfall is dramatic and exciting, both visually and aurally.

Water has a wide variety of practical uses as well. Like all living things, plants and lawns need water to survive and flourish, and in many areas of the country, this is provided by sprinkler systems, which may be designed or specified by the site planner. Water also moderates the microclimate of a site, as discussed in the previous lesson.

The sound of falling water may be used to mask urban noise from cars and other sources, as in Freeway Park in Seattle.

The recreational uses of water are many and varied: swimming in a backyard pool, sailing or waterskiing on a lake, snorkeling in the ocean. The site planner may have to consider the conflicting needs of recreational users, i.e., swimming vs. power boating.

The need for water as recreation may have to be weighed against environmental and other considerations: should a wild river be tamed by damming, or should it be left alone, for scenic enjoyment and whitewater rafting? Some of these decisions are made by the site planner, while others are beyond his or her control. But in any event, the planner should have a thorough understanding of water as a natural resource.

Water in Site Design

Wherever a body of water exists, the land near it is very desirable, and this is reflected in the high price of waterfront property. It seems reasonable, therefore, that any body of water

on a site should be preserved, protected, and enhanced. Let's examine each of these goals.

One should preserve a water body by leaving it and the area surrounding it in the natural, undisturbed state whenever possible. We protect it by preventing any kind of contamination. For example, polluted surface runoff should be treated or filtered before being allowed to flow into a body of water. We also maintain natural drainage channels whenever possible and provide detention swales or ponds to prevent flooding.

How can we enhance a body of water? One way is to limit development along the shoreline, thereby creating attractive open space, as well as a much longer effective shoreline set back from the water.

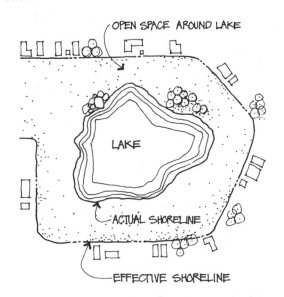

LIMITING SHORELINE DEVELOPMENT
Figure 2.10

Enhancement of an existing lake may also come about when a dam is built. Dams are constructed for a variety of purposes, including flood control and generation of hydroelectric power. One by-product is the creation or enlargement of an upstream lake, which can be used for recreation and as a scenic feature. In recent years, many people have questioned the wisdom of large-scale dam construction, because it inevitably affects, and may even destroy, the natural ecology of an area. Here, as in many other aspects of site and regional planning, one must weigh the advantages and disadvantages of man's intervention in nature.

Just as buildings can become dilapidated through age, use, or misuse, so too some water bodies become unattractive and unappealing: the canals in Venice, California, which were once intended to rival those of their Italian namesake, have fallen into disrepair through neglect. But such water features can be reclaimed and restored.

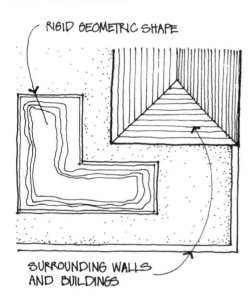

REFLECTION POOL IN URBAN SETTING

Figure 2.11

Where a water body is created or reclaimed, it is often desirable that its shape be natural and curvilinear, rather than artificial and geometric. Of course, this is not always the case. Where manmade forms predominate, as in many urban settings, it is often appropriate for a body of

water introduced into the environment to be rigid in shape and appear man-made.

If possible, the shape of a lake or pond in a rural setting should be such that the entire pond cannot be seen from the shoreline, thus adding to the sense of mystery and the appeal of the pond. Usually, the best sense of balance and harmony is attained when the lake or pond is lower in elevation than any other point in the immediate area.

Paths along the shore should reflect the shape of the pond or lake and the undulation of the water. The design of paths, bridges, docks, and any other structures at the water's edge should be simple and utilize durable and water-resistant materials. Corrosion and weathering are always problems near the water, particularly in the salty atmosphere close to the ocean.

Where possible, banks should be left natural, unless they require surface treatment to withstand the erosive effect of the water.

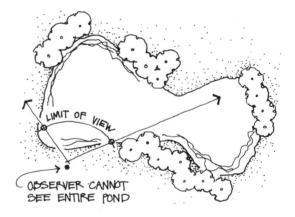

POND IN RURAL SETTING

Figure 2.12

Such surface treatment may consist of stone, reinforced concrete, treated lumber, or steel, always allowing sufficient freeboard (distance from normal water line to the top of the adjacent surface) for the highest expected water level and maximum wave action.

Whatever the size of the site, the use of water as an outdoor design element adds interest and symbolizes refreshment.

Streams

A stream is any body of water flowing in a channel, such as a river or brook. Its flow varies with the year, the season, and the place, but a stream is always part of a natural drainage system, and therefore, it should be disturbed as little as possible. In general, river banks should also be left alone, because reshaping them or removing existing vegetation may increase erosion.

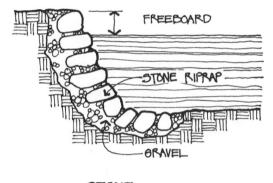

STONE

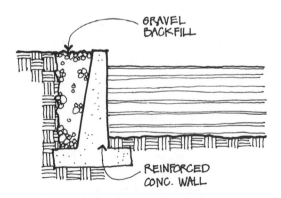

REINFORCED CONCRETE

REINFORCING THE WATER'S EDGE

Figure 2.13

But nature does not always serve man's needs, and sometimes alterations are necessary. For example, rivers must be crossed. Such crossings should be located where they are most feasible structurally: where the stream is narrow, to minimize the length of span; where the banks are stable, so that economical foundations can be constructed; and where the banks are higher than the highest expected flood line.

If a crossing must be made in an area subject to flooding, the bridge members should be designed to resist the dynamic action of flood waters.

Where the span between banks is great, additional piers within the stream may be required. Such piers should be oriented with their long dimension parallel to the direction of flow, to minimize disruption of stream flow and the resulting turbulence.

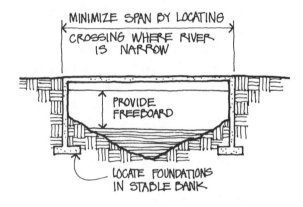

RIVER CROSSING

Figure 2.14

An open manmade drainage channel is also a stream, usually lined with concrete. Such a channel is most efficient if it is straight, without curves or bends, and with a constant width and depth. But a straight channel with a uniform cross-section is not very interesting; a curvilinear channel with a varying cross-section and landscaped banks has a more natural and attractive appearance.

Waterfalls and Fountains

Water falling freely through space because of a sudden change in elevation of its channel creates the most dramatic of all water displays—the waterfall. Natural and manmade waterfalls occur in the outdoor environment in a variety of sizes, shapes, and descriptions. The water may fall in a smooth sheet, or it may be rippled. There may be several falls in segments, or one free fall. And the water may fall into a lake or pool at its base, or onto a hard surface, such as rock.

Each waterfall is unique and creates a different effect. But the interaction of water, light, and sound is always spectacular and always forms a focal point.

The fountain is another dramatic, often theatrical, display of the power of water. Where it is utilized in site design, a large fountain is often the center of attraction, sometimes comprising a variety of jets with multicolored lights and even musical accompaniment. But fountains are not always spectacular—a small, simple fountain, for example, can provide a point of interest in a backyard garden.

Unlike waterfalls, fountains are almost always man-made, with the exception of natural geysers. Regardless of its size or shape, a fountain is perceived as a cool element, making it particularly attractive in a warm, dry climate.

Water Cycle

All the water on the earth, under the ground, and in the atmosphere is part of one unified system, called the hydrologic or water cycle. After water falls on the land as *precipitation*, either rain or snow, it follows three paths. A

small amount flows off the land into streams and eventually into the ocean as *runoff*. A still smaller quantity soaks into the ground as *infiltration*. Most of the precipitation is evaporated into the atmosphere directly and by *transpiration*, through the action of plants, thus completing the cycle.

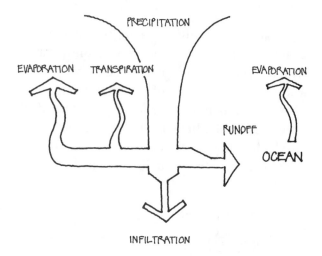

DIAGRAMMATIC WATER CYCLE
Figure 2.15

Runoff therefore consists of total precipitation, less the water infiltrated into the soil, less the water evaporated directly to the air, less the water transpired back to the air from plants, as shown in Figure 2.15.

In site planning, we are concerned with all of these hydrologic processes, particularly runoff and infiltration. When a site is developed, the amount of runoff increases. To understand why this is true, let's look at Figure 2.16. Site development generally entails the removal of some vegetation, thus decreasing the amount of transpiration. Also, relatively pervious land is replaced by impervious buildings, streets, and parking areas, which reduces infiltration. Less transpiration into the air and less infiltration into the soil mean more surface runoff.

How does the site drainage system handle this surface runoff? One approach is for the runoff to immediately enter the drainage system. A different approach requires that most rainfall be held in a *detention pond* on the site until the rain subsides. The runoff is then released slowly without causing flooding. The intent of this second approach, which is often required by local ordinance, is that the flow of rain water from the new development be equal to the runoff from the site prior to development. Sustainable Design would suggest that the second approach is more environmentally appropriate. In fact, it would encourage the slopes of the ponds to be covered in wetland vegetation to allow the entering waters to be naturally filtered.

Potential Flooding

We have said that the development of a site increases the amount of runoff. On a larger scale, urbanization has a similar effect on the hydrologic cycle: the amount and speed of runoff are increased, the runoff is warmer and contains pollutants, and the stream which eventually carries the runoff is visually impaired as a result of erosion and pollution. Urbanization in this country has been especially rapid during the past 30 years. Consequently, there have been a number of disastrous floods. Although measures have been taken by various public agencies, the potential danger of flooding remains high in some areas.

The relatively flat land within which a stream flows is called a *floodplain*. When the volume of flow exceeds the stream's capacity, it overflows its banks and spreads onto the floodplain. This occurs regularly, and the boundary of the flooded area depends on the flood frequency. Thus a ten-year flood inundates less land than a 100-year flood.

The term ten-year flood refers to a flood of a magnitude such that it is likely to occur only once every ten years; therefore, the likelihood of a ten-year flood occurring in any given year is ten percent. Similarly, a 100-year flood is one that is expected to occur once every 100 years. A 100-year flood therefore has a much greater magnitude than a ten-year flood. When designing in flood-prone areas, we select a flood of a

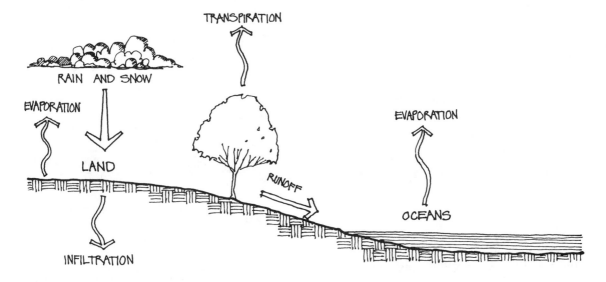

THE WATER CYCLE

Figure 2.16

given magnitude—say a 100-year flood—and set floor elevations above that flood level.

Since the floodplain is subject to natural and recurring floods, it seems obvious that any construction within the floodplain courts disaster. Therefore, such lands should be limited to open space uses, such as recreation and agriculture. This swath of land can provide a natural, park-like, easily maintained setting. Unfortunately, it doesn't always work out that way; as desirable land for development becomes scarcer and more expensive, there is increased pressure to build on floodplains. As a compromise, low-density housing is often permitted, provided the occupants are aware of the potential hazard and the structures are elevated above flood level.

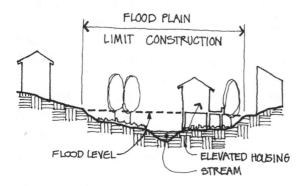

SECTION THROUGH FLOOD PLAIN
Figure 2.17

The water table in a floodplain usually occurs near the surface, drainage is generally poor, and the soil deep and uniform. The soil is often subject to large volumetric changes when it becomes wet, making it unsatisfactory for supporting building loads, but usually excellent for agriculture. The rivers in floodplains are often meandering.

The conventional solution to the problem of potential flooding involves the construction of concrete channels. Alternatively, existing natural drainage channels and floodplains can be utilized, even if some modifications are

required. Such solutions preserve the aesthetics and ecology of the natural environment and are compatible with the Sustainable Design philosophy.

Underground Water

The water contained in the voids and crevices under the earth's surface exceeds by far all of the water contained in streams and lakes. This underground water comes from precipitation, both rain and snow, which soaks directly into the ground or drains into rivers and lakes and then seeps into the ground.

Underground water is found either in the zone of aeration or the zone of saturation. The zone of aeration is the higher zone, where the spaces between the soil grains contain both water and air. In the lower zone, the zone of saturation, all of the void spaces are filled completely with ground water. The irregular surface which forms the boundary between the two zones is called the *ground water table*. This is usually a sloping surface which fluctuates seasonally and roughly follows the ground surface.

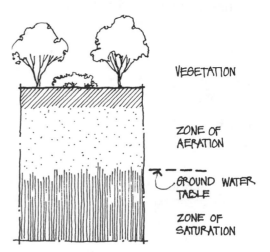

UNDERGROUND WATER ZONES
Figure 2.18

Where the ground water table is high, about six feet below the surface, construction excavation must be braced and kept dry by pumping. Basements must be waterproofed, basement walls designed to resist hydrostatic pressure, underground tanks or other structures designed to resist uplift, and the bearing capacity of the foundation soils often reduced.

Underground water flows at a very slow velocity, depending on the porosity and permeability of the underground earth or rock material. An underground permeable material through which water flows is called an *aquifer*. Sand, gravel, sandstone, and some limestones are generally good aquifers, while clay, shale, and most metamorphic and igneous rocks are poor aquifers.

PLANTS

Introduction

Plants are an important site design element and provide beauty and vitality to the outdoor environment. A site development without plants would be like a moonscape—stark and lifeless. Plants soften the hard edges, define spaces, and add interest.

The use of planting in site design is not merely ornamental or decorative, any more than a building design is. Rather, the site planner often considers planting as a functional element and an integral part of the overall design of the site. In fact, indigenous planting is usually easier to maintain and often provides functional benefits such as filtering storm water or providing habitat for local wildlife.

Plants are unique in that they are the only design element that is alive and hence ever-changing. They grow, change with the seasons, and move with the winds. The site planner must be aware of seasonal characteristics and growth patterns, and realize that the plant that is placed in the ground today will look different next month and next year.

Other design elements can often be ignored after a site is developed, but plants, being alive, need constant nurturing; they need the right soil, sun and wind exposure, temperature range, moisture, and nutrients to live and thrive. The site planner considers this need for ongoing maintenance and often selects plant materials that are relatively easy to care for. On the other hand, where proper maintenance of vegetation is simply too difficult or expensive to achieve, other elements, sometimes inferior, are used as substitutes—for example, blacktop paving instead of grass in a school yard.

Like all natural things, plants are imperfect and not totally predictable. That is the essence of their appeal: they provide a connection with nature.

Defining Space

When we speak of plants or vegetation in this lesson, we are referring to all living organisms in the environment which draw their sustenance from the soil. Trees, shrubs, ground cover, lawn—all are plants. Our discussion comprises both indigenous vegetation and plants introduced into the environment. Since native plants, by their very existence, are well suited to a site, they should be preserved, unless there is an overriding reason to remove them.

New plants should not be introduced haphazardly, but only after careful consideration. A well thought out landscape can change an ordinary site into one that is attractive and distinctive.

In addition to their aesthetic value, plants serve a variety of other functions in the outdoor environment, including defining space.

In a building, space is usually defined by rigid physical elements, such as walls, ceiling, and floor. Outside, the definition of space is more subtle. Trees or shrubs may provide a feeling of vertical enclosure, without actually enclosing an area. With deciduous trees, the spatial definition is much stronger in the summer than in the winter, when the trees have lost their foliage. Closely spaced trees may also provide a horizontal enclosure, or ceiling.

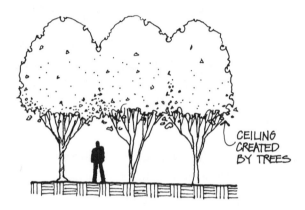

TREES CREATE HORIZONTAL ENCLOSURE
Figure 2.19

In addition to forming enclosures, trees may visually connect structural elements, such as buildings, and direct people into a space. Thus, the site planner can create a variety of spatial feelings through the use of plants.

Plants can act as a screening device; a cluster of tall, dense trees may provide privacy for an outdoor terrace, for example.

While the trees block the view into the terrace, they also prevent viewing from the terrace, and thus separate it from its surroundings.

Unattractive site elements may be visually screened by planting: most people would rather look at trees than mechanical equipment or parked cars.

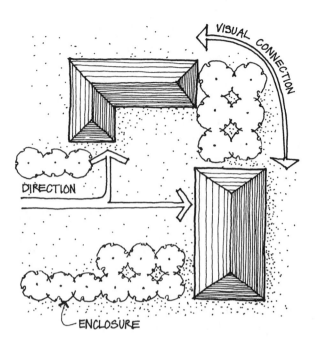

TREES ENCLOSE, DIRECT, AND CONNECT
Figure 2.20

Of course, planting used for privacy or screening should be evergreen, in order to be effective throughout the year.

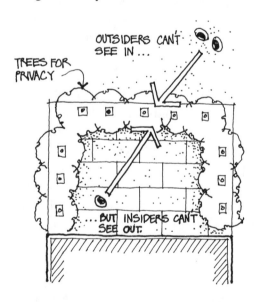

PRIVACY CREATES SEPARATION
Figure 2.21

Environmental Control

Vegetation is one of the most moderating influences on the environment. Trees block both the sun and the wind. They act as nature's air conditioning by cooling, humidifying, and filtering the air. They create sheltered zones by reducing wind speeds.

Trees and other planting help to control erosion, destructive runoff, and flooding. They absorb sound. And they provide a habitat for birds.

In these and other ways, plants improve the quality of the environment and hence, the quality of human life.

Aesthetics

For convenience, we have separated the various functions of plants. In reality, of course, all of these functions may be performed simultaneously; a tree can provide shade, help to define space, and look beautiful, all at the same time.

Trees are the dominant plant material; they must be carefully selected and placed to assure a successful design. In general, trees should be clustered as they are in nature, and not spaced too regularly or too far apart. A row of uniformly spaced trees tends to look formal and unnatural; however, it may be appropriate along a street or in an urban setting, to reflect the rigid forms of the built environment.

Occasionally, a single tree can be used as a focal point in the outdoor environment, in much the same way as a piece of sculpture. It may stand by itself, or it may be complemented by smaller trees and plants to create a unified composition.

While the larger trees are dominant, smaller trees and shrubs are used to subdivide the site into smaller areas, visually connect the various

site elements, define paths or roads, and add visual interest.

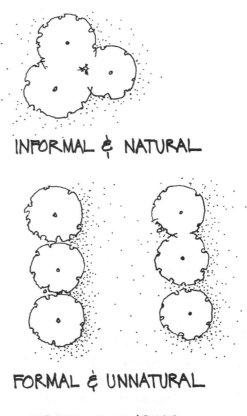

INFORMAL & NATURAL

FORMAL & UNNATURAL

TREE GROUPINGS
Figure 2.22

If we think of larger plant materials forming the walls and ceiling of the outside environment, then ground cover is its carpet. Ground cover defines a space or surface, provides visual interest because of its color or texture, and retains soil and moisture.

Trees or other plant materials may be used to frame a view.

Just as the facade of a building should be free from clutter, without too many materials or fussy details, so too one should avoid the use of numerous plant varieties and complex groupings. It's best to keep it simple, using just a few carefully chosen, grouped, and placed plant varieties.

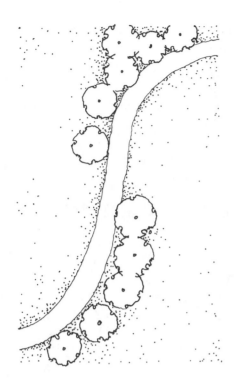

SHRUBS DEFINE A PATH
Figure 2.23

However, this does not mean that only one plant size or form should be used. There is an almost infinite variety of sizes, forms, textures, and colors of plants to choose from. In general, most of the plants in a site design should be more or less conventional and appropriate to their surroundings. However, plants of varied shapes, colors, and textures may be added to provide more interest. Too little variation is dull and monotonous, while too much is busy and even chaotic.

SOIL

Soil Composition

The stability of a building depends on the bearing capacity of the soil upon which it sits. The composition of soil is almost infinite in its variety, ranging from bedrock to loose organic material. While rock can easily support the enormous weight of multistory structures (as in midtown Manhattan), loose, wet sand may be incapable of supporting even a small animal unlucky enough to be caught in quicksand.

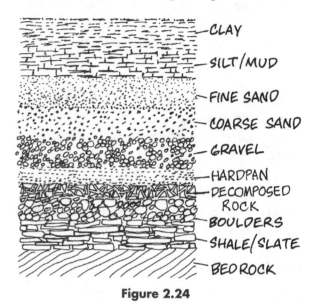

Figure 2.24

Soil composition determines a soil's bearing capacity. Soil is formed by the chemical decomposition of rock; water, air, and temperature action on rock; and the decay of vegetable and animal matter. A variety of these processes has resulted in the top layer of the earth's surface. Although the soil composition at a particular site is unique, soil types throughout the world are essentially similar, and they are identified in most soil classifications as bedrock, boulders, decomposed rock, hardpan, gravel, sand, silt, clay, and quicksand, or as mixtures of more than one soil type.

Soil Types

Rock, often referred to as *bedrock*, is the solid material that forms the crust of the earth. It is generally the strongest support for the foundation of a structure. *Slate* and *shale* are fine-textured soft rock. *Boulders* are rock detached from the bedrock of which they were once a part, and *decomposed rock* refers to disintegrated rock masses that were originally solid.

Hardpan is a consolidated mixture of gravel, clay, and sand, and it is a good foundation base for buildings.

Gravel consists of granular rock particles ranging in size from 1/4 inch to 3-1/2 inch. Any rock pieces that are larger are called cobblestones, and if still larger, boulders.

Sand consists of loose granular rock particles about .002 inch to 1/4 inch in size. Sand is neither plastic nor cohesive in its pure state. Sand and gravel are coarse-grained soils that provide an excellent base for building foundations, as well as excellent drainage properties, as they are relatively permeable.

Silt is a fine-grained sedimentary material deposited from running water. It is .002 inch or less in particle size. When mixed with water, it forms a soft, plastic, sticky material known as mud.

Clay is a fine-grained, firm cohesive material formed from the decomposition and hydration of certain rock. Clay is plastic when wet and relatively hard when dry. Clay is relatively impervious, and it may swell when it absorbs water and shrink when it dries, making it the least stable and predictable soil for the support of buildings. Clays and silts may provide satisfactory support for building foundations, but they require careful investigation.

Quicksand is a mixture of sand and moving water that is completely unsuitable for construction and a danger to any object falling, stepping, or resting on its surface.

Table 2.2 shows allowable soil pressures. It is reproduced from the Uniform Building Code (UBC). Soil bearing values from other sources are similar.

TABLE 18-I-A – ALLOWABLE FOUNDATION AND LATERAL PRESSURE

CLASS OF MATERIALS[1]	ALLOWABLE FOUNDATION PRESSURE (psf)[2] × 0.0479 for kPa	LATERAL BEARING LBS./SQ./FT./FT. OF DEPTH BELOW NATURAL GRADE[3] × 0.157 for kPa per meter	LATERAL SLIDING[4] Coefficient[5]	Resistance (psf)[6] × 0.0479 for kPa
1. Massive crystalline bedrock	4,000	1,200	.70	
2. Sedimentary and foliated rock	2,000	400	.35	
3. Sandy gravel and/or gravel (GW and GP)	2,000	200	.35	
4. Sand, silty sand, clayey sand, silty gravel and clayey gravel (SW, SP, SM, SC, GM and GC)	1,500	150	.25	
5. Clay, sandy clay, silty clay and clayey silt (CL, ML, MH and CH)	1,000[7]	100		130

[1]For soil classifications OL, OH and PT (i.e., organic clays and peat), a foundation investigation shall be required.
[2]All values of allowable foundation pressure are for footings having a minimum width of 12 inches (305 mm) and a minimum depth of 12 inches (305 mm) into natural grade. Except as in Footnote 7 below, increase of 20 percent allowed for each additional foot (305 mm) of width or depth to a maximum value of three times the designated value.
[3]May be increased the amount of the designated value for each additional foot (305 mm) of depth to a maximum of 15 times the designated value. Isolated poles for uses such as flagpoles or signs and poles used to support buildings which are not adversely affected by a 1/2-inch (13 mm) motion at ground surface due to short-term lateral loads may be designed using lateral bearing values equal to two times the tabulated values.
[4]Lateral bearing and lateral sliding resistance may be combined.
[5]Coefficient to be multiplied by the dead load.
[6]Lateral sliding resistance value to be multiplied by the contact area. In no case shall the lateral sliding resistance exceed one half the dead load.
[7]No increase for width is allowed.

Reprinted from *Uniform Building Code*, copyright International Conference of Building Officials, Whittier, California, 1997. All rights reserved.

Table 2.2

SOIL EXPLORATION AND TESTING

To understand a site's soil conditions, the architect generally requests a subsurface exploration of the site. Unless the entire site is an obvious outcrop of rock, guesswork is not advisable. More than one architect has excavated through firm-looking material only to discover alluvial silt or uncompacted fill extending down 10 or 20 feet or more.

There are a variety of soil exploration methods in common use, each of which may be appropriate, depending on the location, topography, depth of water table, and particularly on the magnitude of the structural loads anticipated. The test pit and soil load tests are two relatively uncomplicated methods that offer immediate results. Other tests that rely on boring into the earth include auger borings, wash borings, core borings, and dry sample borings.

Test Pits

Test pits are simple excavations that permit direct visual inspection of the actual soil conditions. Open pits allow close-up examination of the soil layers, as well as access to undisturbed samples for further laboratory testing. Excavating test pits to any substantial depth is costly, and they are generally not dug below the water table.

Soil Load Tests

Soil load tests employing a loading platform are empirical in nature and as old as the art of foundation design. A platform is erected on the site and incremental loads are applied; each load increment is maintained until the settlement becomes negligible for a period of several hours. The test continues until the measured settlement becomes regular under subsequent

loadings. The total test load is usually double the contemplated design load.

Borings

Auger borings are designed to bring up soil samples by means of an ordinary 2- or 2-1/2-inch auger fastened to a long pipe or rod. The auger usually stops at the first obstruction, which may be rock, hardpan, or the stump of a tree. This method is most effective in sand or clay and for depths not exceeding 50 feet.

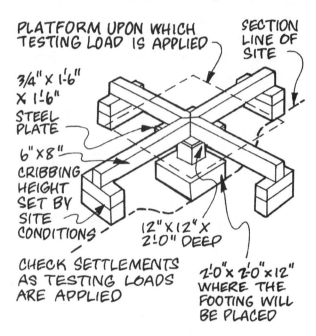

LOADING PLATFORM
Figure 2.25

Wash borings are useful in locating bedrock when the soil is too compact to use an auger. These borings are made with a two- to four-inch diameter pipe that is driven into the soil and contains a smaller jet pipe through which water is forced. The material washed up is often thoroughly mixed, thus reducing the dependability of the samples. Another problem in the use of wash borings is that boulders may be mistaken for bedrock. This system can penetrate all other materials, however, and the test can be extended downward 100 feet or more.

Core borings are more costly than most other methods, but they are the most reliable. They can penetrate through all materials, to great depths, and bring up complete cores of the material through which they pass. Core borings are made with a diamond drill that is sufficiently hard to cut through rock. The results of these borings are usually recorded, according to standard practices, in a test boring log book, shown in Table 2.3.

Dry sample borings utilize a drive pipe with a special split sampling pipe at the tip instead of a drill. The sampling pipe is driven down approximately five inches, then lifted out, and the contents removed and stored. Soil samples are taken every five inches, and the removed soil is tested in a laboratory.

With each of the methods above, it is important to check a sufficient number of locations over the building area in order to determine the depth and extent of good bearing material. For large structures, a site plan with the building outline is often used by a structural engineer to indicate the number, size, and location of the test borings to be made. Soil analysis is performed by a soils engineer or agency that is generally subject to approval by the local building department.

Soil Properties

Some properties for which soil may be tested include the following:

Specific gravity, to determine void ratio.

Grain size (for granular soils), to estimate permeability, frost action, compaction, and shear strength.

Grain shape, to estimate shear strength.

Liquid and plastic limits (in cohesive soils), to obtain compressibility and compaction values.

Water content (in cohesive soils), to obtain compressibility and compaction values.

Void ratio, to determine compressibility.

Unconfined compression (in cohesive soils), to estimate shear strength.

Based on the field exploration and laboratory tests, a written soils report is prepared in which the soils engineer recommends the type of foundation to be used and the allowable soil bearing pressure.

SOIL AND SITE PROBLEMS

There are enough problems on the earth's crust to ruin the good night's sleep of many an architect. These soil problems may involve inadequate bearing capacity, subsurface water, shrinkage, slippage, and—in some parts of the country—unpredictable earth movement due to seismic forces. Architects like to think of the earth as stable, just as clients prefer to think of their buildings as immovable; the fact is, however, that neither is permanently fixed forever.

Settlement

Settlement of buildings must be carefully considered, except when the structure's foundations are on solid bedrock where little or no settlement can occur. As dead load is added to the structure, it compresses the soil beneath the footings, reducing the void volume and causing settlement.

A slight amount of settlement that is uniform throughout the structure is of little concern.

TYPICAL PAGE FROM TEST BORING LOG BOOK

BORING LOG NO. 5

Drilling date: September 10, 1997   Elevation: 597

DEPTH IN FEET	DESIGNATION	DESCRIPTION
1	GM	FILL: Silty Gravel, dark grey-brown, very moist, loose
	GM	ALLUVIUM: Silty Gravel, light grey-brown, moist, medium dense
	SC	Clayey Sand layer, light grey-brown, moist, dense, porous
5	GM	continues Silty Gravel, coarser, drier 2' diameter boulder
10	GC	WEATHERED BEDROCK: Clayey gravel, light brown, damp, very dense, grades to Slate Bedrock at 10 feet
		End at 10.0 feet No water, no caving

Note: The designations GM, SC, etc. are standard classification symbols that are in general use. For example, GM indicates silty gravel, or a gravel-sand-silt mixture.

Table 2.3

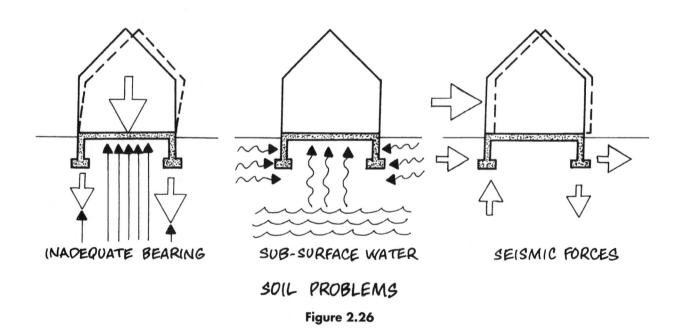

INADEQUATE BEARING   SUB-SURFACE WATER   SEISMIC FORCES

SOIL PROBLEMS

Figure 2.26

However, uneven or *differential settlement* may cause serious cracks or even failures. While a building is under construction, constant checking with surveying instruments should be performed to note any settlement and make certain that it is uniform.

For a number of reasons, settlement may continue for several years after a building is completed. Some soils take a long time to consolidate, the moisture content of the soil may change, or movement may occur within the earth itself.

Frost Action

In cold climates, the freezing and subsequent thawing of soil may cause the ground to heave. This places stress on a building's foundation, which can lead to serious damage.

The extent of frost action depends on the soil type and geographic location. In all areas subject to frost action, footings must be placed at least one foot below the *frost line*, which is the depth below which the soil does not freeze. Frost line levels vary throughout the country, ranging from zero in San Diego to more than six feet in Fargo, North Dakota.

Earth Movement

Earth movement is a prevalent condition with clay subsoils, as clay may swell when wet and shrink when dried. Near the surface, where variations in moisture are common, there may be considerable earth movement. At a depth of about five feet, however, movement will be slight. Thus, serious structural problems can result where some footings are close to the ground surface and other footings are quite deep.

The moisture content of clay may be affected by an adjacent excavation. This could cause settlement or slippage of the subsurface clay,

either of which can lead to serious damage. Sloping layers of earth may also cause problems, as they tend to move as a mass when subjected to excessive rain or moisture. Evidence of this phenomenon can be seen in older structures that have a slight tilt, or in rows of sloping power poles.

SOIL DRAINAGE

Many severe soil problems are caused by the presence of moisture, both at and below grade. The presence of moisture can lead to reduction of a soil's load bearing capacity, leakage of water into a building, or disintegration of certain building materials. Therefore, the location of subsurface water and the control of surface water must both be considered prior to beginning any construction.

Water Table

The level below which all soil is saturated with ground water is known as the water table. In general, the water table roughly follows the ground surface, but its level may fluctuate because of seasonal variations, precipitation, or developmental changes on the ground surface, such as paving a large parking area.

In practice, building foundations should be located well above the site's water table to avoid potential damage from hydrostatic pressure or capillary action. In addition, subsurface water should be diverted away from the foundation by means of a drain tile system. Drainage tiles have a minimum diameter of six inches and are laid in gravel, or another kind of porous bed, at least six inches below the lowest floor slab. Open joints between tiles should be covered with wire screening to prevent clogging, and then covered by coarse gravel or stone backfill.

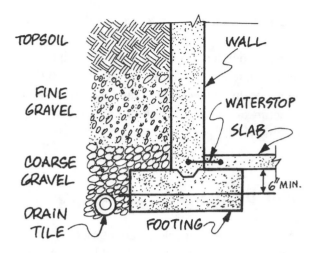

TOPSOIL

FINE GRAVEL

COARSE GRAVEL

DRAIN TILE

WALL

WATERSTOP

SLAB

6" MIN.

FOOTING

DRAINAGE TILE INSTALLATION
Figure 2.27

Slabs on grade not subject to hydrostatic pressure are often placed over a gravel fill several inches thick, which prevents water from being drawn into the slab by capillary action.

In place of solid pipes laid with open joints, round or half-round drainage tiles with perforations on the bottom may be used.

A preformed *waterstop* may be used between the slab on grade and the foundation wall to seal the joint against water penetration.

Drainage

Drainage of surface water involves directing water away from all structures. This is accomplished by grading or shaping the contours of the site to provide a gradual transition from high to low elevations. Gutters, flumes, berms, and the gentle warp of paved surfaces collect and conduct water to yard drains, catch basins, and underground storm drainage lines from which it is finally discharged.

SOIL MODIFICATION

Soil can be altered in a variety of ways in order to improve its consistency, dependability, and bearing capacity. Under normal conditions, bearing capacity may be increased by simply deepening or increasing the bearing area of the footing. Drainage is another common method used to improve the physical characteristics of soil, especially where the soil is affected by subterranean water flow.

If the subsoil is unusually soft or contains organic fill, the undesirable material should be removed and replaced with compacted granular materials. If this excavation and replacement process is too costly, other methods of soil consolidation may be used. For example, a compressible soil can be improved by covering it with a porous layer of sand, gravel, or crushed rock and blending it into the natural material. Thus, hardpan-type soil material can be artificially produced.

Because density of soil is a rough measure of its strength, soil improvement often involves a reduction in the void volume. This can be achieved by adding a compacted layer of cinders or ash, by subsurface drainage, or by the ancient method of using a large number of short piles in the ground to compress the upper layer of the earth.

Soils may also be compacted by the use of heavy machinery, such as sheepsfoot rollers. In such cases, the control of density can be critical. Overcompaction will improve soil strength, but it may produce an unstable structure within the soil, resulting in serious heaving of the earth.

All soil modification methods intended to increase load-bearing capacity should be reviewed by the local building department prior to starting any work.

TOPOGRAPHY AND DRAINAGE

Topography

An analysis of a building site is necessary in order to determine which areas are most suitable for specific uses, such as buildings, roads and paths, and parking areas. Building placement, parking area layout, and drainage are among the factors that may suggest regrading of the land.

The regraded land should be functional and as harmonious as possible with the existing landscape. Where possible, cut and fill should be balanced in order to avoid the expense of either importing or exporting soil.

Drainage

Similarly, the drainage patterns of the site must be analyzed. On-site drainage systems must be connected to existing natural drainage systems. If, as is often the case, the building development interrupts or alters the existing natural drainage system, that system must not be blocked, nor should the flow that it is required to handle be increased without increasing the system's capacity. Design of such drainage patterns is called *surface water management.*

Storm water that does not seep into the ground is called runoff, and it must be drained away from buildings, roads, and other areas of activity in a proper manner in order to prevent flooding or erosion. The design of a surface drainage system is based on the amount of runoff to be carried, which in turn is determined by the intensity and duration of a storm, the size of the area drained, and the characteristics of the drained area, such as soil porosity, slope, and vegetation cover. The rate of surface water runoff increases as streets, paving, parking areas, and roofs replace the existing natural ground surface. The design of a surface water drain-

age system is based on the most severe storm expected once every 5, 10, or, possibly, 25 or more years. A 5-year storm might be used for a residential development, while a 25- or 50-year storm might be the basis for a shopping center or other extensively developed project.

Drainage Systems

The drainage system may consist of a surface "sheet flow" system, surface flow in gutters, or flow in underground pipes. Water will flow as a sheet across the surface of a paved or planted area when the slope is between one-half of one percent and one percent. The land adjacent to a building should be sloped away at a grade of at least 2 percent. Drainage ditches should be sloped a minimum of 2 percent to a maximum of 10 percent, grass slopes should not exceed a 25 percent grade, and the slope of unmowed ground cover, such as ivy, may be as steep as 50 percent if the soil is stable. Slopes greater than 50 percent should be avoided due to the likelihood of erosion caused by extremely raped runoff, which can be slowed by interrupting the flow with "check dams." Finished ground surfaces should always have positive drainage and be free of undrained depressions, since these may cause water stagnation.

To avoid erosion, surface flow is often concentrated in channels, which may be paved gutters or grass swales. These channels, in turn, drain into natural drainage channels or connect to underground storm drainage systems.

Underground drainage conduits should be sufficiently sloped to be self-cleansing, normally a minimum of 0.3 percent. They should be placed at an adequate depth below the ground surface to avoid damage by vehicles and to prevent freezing, which may occur as deep as three to four feet in the colder climates. Excessively deep excavation or excavation in rock will, of course, increase site development cost, possibly to the point where it is prohibitive. On very steep ground, storm drains and sanitary sewers may require special internal design to prevent scouring action or, in extreme cases, destructive wear on interior conduit surfaces.

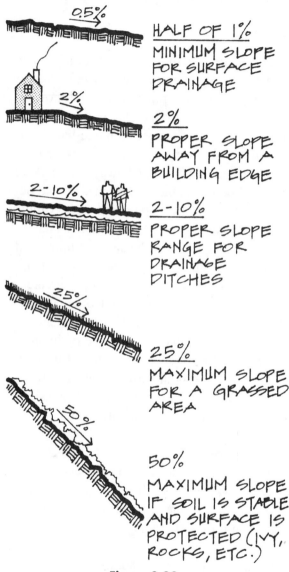

Figure 2.28

For obvious reasons of economy, surface drainage is preferable to underground storm drainage systems, that is, grading should always be kept to a minimum. If storm drains are necessary, the layout should be simple, with a minimum length of drain lines, as few access manholes as possible, and minimum disruption of the natural conditions. Sustainable design emphasizes infrastructure such as swales for surface drainage, which not only carry water but also contain native wetland vegetation that filters and cleans the storm water as it moves through the grasses.

Underground water may be carried in subsurface drain lines with open joints, which allows water in the soil to be drained. The amount of water flow into these drains is determined by the permeability of the soil, the depth of the drain, the size of the drain, and the size and spacing of the joints or perforations in the drain pipes. Drainage lines are made of clay tile or of plastic (PVC), and require adequate slope similar to storm drains.

Ground Slope

Ground surface slopes are generally classified as *level*, *easy grades*, and *steep grades*. Slopes under 4 percent appear nearly level to the eye, and are suitable for construction and outdoor activities of every type. Slopes between 4 and 10 percent are easy grades and are suitable for most construction and activity. Steep grades, over 10 percent, are more difficult to use and consequently, more expensive for building construction because of complicated foundations and utility connections. A sloping site often lends itself to a split-level design solution. There are, of course, numerous other design possibilities available to the designer for accommodating a structure to a steeply sloping site.

The maximum desirable slope of grassy recreational areas is 3 percent, walks adjacent to buildings should not exceed a 4 percent slope, the slope of parking areas should be limited to 5 percent, and streets used by vehicles should not exceed a slope of 10 percent.

Understanding Topography

Topography refers to the surface features of an area. By analyzing topography one can determine building locations, road systems, utility systems, and surface water drainage patterns.

Topographic maps, prepared by surveyors or civil engineers, indicate the topography of the earth's surface, usually by contour lines. Each contour denotes a particular elevation. The change in elevation between two adjacent contours is called the contour interval.

For hilly terrain, larger contour intervals are used, while areas that are relatively flat use closer contour intervals. For legibility, the smaller the scale of the map, the larger the *contour interval.*

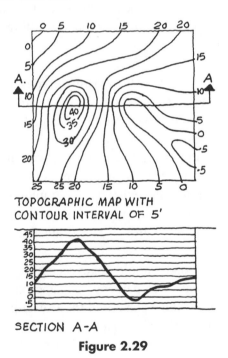

TOPOGRAPHIC MAP WITH
CONTOUR INTERVAL OF 5'

SECTION A-A

Figure 2.29

Ground slope is extremely important in determining site utilization. A convenient way to measure ground slope is by percentage. If h is horizontal distance, v is vertical distance, and g is grade in percent:

$$g = \frac{v}{h} \times 100$$

For example, if the horizontal distance is 40 feet and the vertical distance is 10 feet:

$$g = \frac{10}{40} \times 100 = 25\%$$

Grades under 4 percent are considered flat and therefore suitable for all types of activity. Slopes between 4 and 10 percent are considered to be moderate and require considerable effort to climb or descend. Buildings on such slopes may require complex, and therefore expensive, foundations, and utilities and roads are also likely to be more complex and expensive. Grades of 10 to 50 percent are steep and may be unusable, or suitable for limited activity only. Turfed slopes should be kept under 25 percent to facilitate mowing and maintenance.

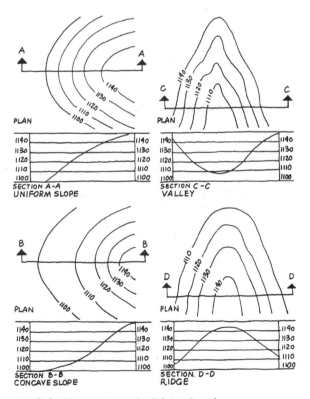

CONTOUR MAPS WITH CONTOUR INTERVALS OF 10'

Figure 2.30

Slopes exceeding 50 percent are very steep, not suitable for any activity, and subject to surface water erosion. At the other extreme, unpaved slopes less than 1 percent do not drain well.

If a slope is too steep (or too flat), regrading may be required. The cost of grading may be excessive, and therefore the development of a site for certain purposes may not be economically feasible.

The designer's task is to analyze the slope pattern and determine the best land uses for various parts of the site, and to locate various developments on the site.

4% SLOPE - INTENSIVE ACTIVITY

4% TO 10% SLOPE- INFORMAL ACTIVITY

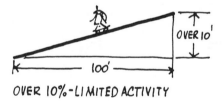

OVER 10% - LIMITED ACTIVITY

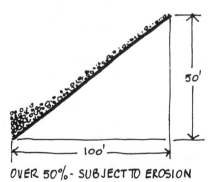

OVER 50% - SUBJECT TO EROSION

Figure 2.31

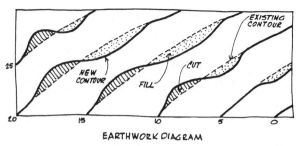

EARTHWORK DIAGRAM

Figure 2.32

If the physical development of a site requires topographic modification, which is often the case, a grading plan is prepared, showing existing and new contours, from which the required amount of earth cutting and filling may be computed.

In general, changes in natural topography should be kept to a minimum. If grading is required, however, the amount of cutting should approximately equal the amount of filling, if possible.

Grading plans show the existing grades at property boundaries, as well as the grades for the site's structures, roads, and landscape features.

Ground form also influences the layout of roads, sanitary sewers, and storm drains. Some modification to the existing topography is usually necessary in order to lay out roads and utilities and to control surface drainage.

Generally, roads should not exceed a ten percent gradient. A 15 percent slope approaches the limit a vehicle can climb for a sustained period. The following is a list of generally accepted gradient standards for certain activities:

Storm drains	0.3% minimum
Sanitary sewers	0.4% to 1.4% (depending on pipe size)
Street drainage (surface)	0.5% minimum (rarely 0.25%)
Open land drainage (some ponding)	0.5% minimum
Planted areas, large paved areas	1% minimum
Drainage ditches, canals	2% minimum, 10% maximum
Parking areas	5% maximum
Automobile ramps— down (grade separations)	8% maximum
Paved walkways, side- walks	10% maximum, 15% for short ramps
Streets, paved drives	10% maximum, 17% for trucks in low gear
Lawns	25% maximum
Planted banks (unmowed)	50% maximum, depending on stability of soil

SITE PREPARATION

Prior to construction, a site must be cleared of all undesirable materials. These might include existing structures that must be demolished, their footings and foundation walls, and existing utility lines that must be disconnected, capped, or relocated.

Plant material that is to remain undisturbed must be protected. Other vegetation must be removed, and root systems and tree stumps must be completely dug out, or grubbed,

because in time they will decay and leave undesirable voids in the ground.

Corner stakes, placed in the ground to locate building lines, may be moved or lost when the excavation begins. Therefore, batter boards, which are offset from the building line, are often used instead. The structure is thus located by means of strings or wires stretched between batter boards, shown in Figure 2.33.

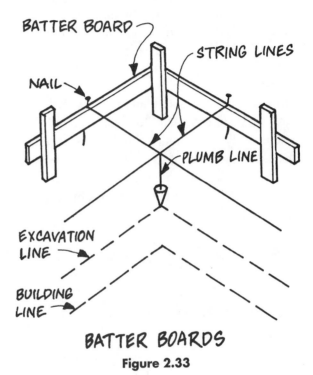

BATTER BOARDS
Figure 2.33

Before grading begins, the top six inches or so of soil (topsoil) are removed and stockpiled on the site. At the conclusion of construction, this topsoil is spread over the area as a final landscape base, which forms the finish grade. On sites where the topsoil is not worth saving, such material may have to be imported at the end of construction.

EARTHWORK

Earthwork consists of all grading work, including excavation, rough grading, and finish grading.

Excavation

Excavation is the removal of existing soil to permit construction of the foundation and substructure. Excavation may be performed by hand or more generally by machines, and includes the digging of basements, trenching for footings, and all other required removal of soil.

Permanently cut slopes should not exceed a slope of 1-1/2 horizontal to 1 vertical, and permanently filled slopes should be no steeper than 2 to 1, unless substantiated by soil tests or geological data. A cubic yard of earth weighs more than a ton, and therefore unstable earth slopes represent a danger that must be avoided or corrected.

Grading

Grading is the alteration of a site's contours, usually by means of power equipment. *Rough grading* is the addition or removal of earth prior to the start of construction. *Finish grading* is the final distribution of earth at the conclusion of construction. It is generally a more precise operation and may include the placement of topsoil for landscaping. Finish grades are usually accurate to within one inch and represent the final shaping of a site's contours.

Backfill

Backfill is earth that is replaced around a foundation or retaining wall after the concrete forms have been removed. Backfill material should be deposited in layers 6 to 12 inches in

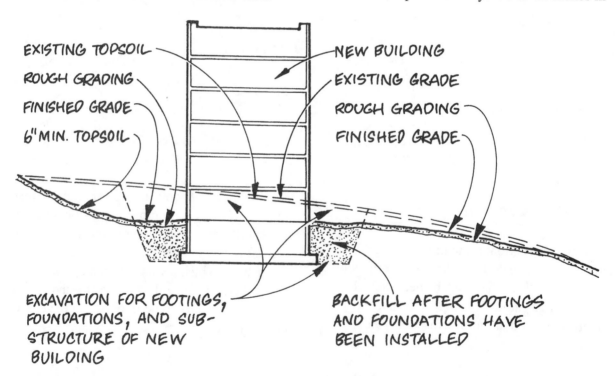

EXISTING TOPSOIL
ROUGH GRADING
FINISHED GRADE
6" MIN. TOPSOIL

NEW BUILDING
EXISTING GRADE
ROUGH GRADING
FINISHED GRADE

EXCAVATION FOR FOOTINGS, FOUNDATIONS, AND SUB-STRUCTURE OF NEW BUILDING

BACKFILL AFTER FOOTINGS AND FOUNDATIONS HAVE BEEN INSTALLED

EXCAVATION, ROUGH AND FINISH GRADING, AND BACKFILL

Figure 2.34

depth and thoroughly tamped and compacted to avoid settlement. Backfill used over drain lines should be devoid of rock or other material that could crack or displace tiles. It should also be free of any debris that might later disintegrate and form voids.

FOUNDATIONS

The *foundation* of a building is the part of its structure that transmits the building's loads to the soil, while *footings* are those parts of a foundation that are widened to spread the load over a large area of soil.

In every case, the load of a building must not exceed the safe bearing capacity of the underlying soil, in order to avoid distress such as settlement cracks, uneven structural movement, or even failure of the structure.

Shallow Foundations

If the soils close to the ground are of adequate strength, the most economical foundation system generally consists of shallow spread footings, of which there are several basic types. A *column footing* is a square or rectangular pad of concrete that spreads the column load over a sufficiently large area so that the bearing capacity of the soil is not exceeded. A *wall footing* is a continuous spread footing that serves the same purpose under a wall. When a column footing abuts the property line, a *combined footing* or a *cantilever footing* may be used that connects the exterior column footing to the first interior column footing. A *mat footing* is essentially one large footing under the entire building that distributes the load over the entire building area. Also called a *raft foundation*, it is used when soil conditions are poor. A *boat footing* is similar to a mat footing, except that it is placed at a depth such that the weight of the soil removed from the excavation is equal

to the load of the building, and thus little or no new load is added to the underlying soil.

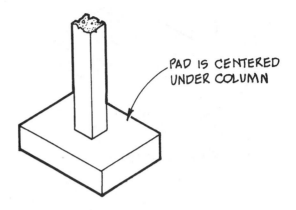

PAD IS CENTERED UNDER COLUMN

COLUMN FOOTING
Figure 2.35

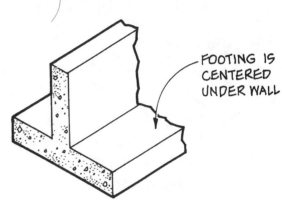

FOOTING IS CENTERED UNDER WALL

WALL FOOTING
Figure 2.36

Deep Foundations

If the upper soils have insufficient bearing capacity to support spread footings, the building loads are often transmitted to deeper, firmer soils by *piles*, which are driven into the ground.

A pile may transfer the load to the soil by skin friction between the pile and the surrounding soil, or by end bearing, where the load is supported by the rock or firm subsoil under the pile tip.

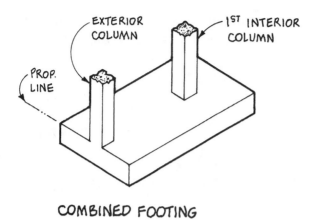

COMBINED FOOTING

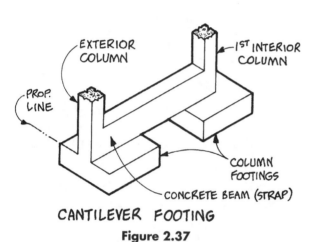

CANTILEVER FOOTING

Figure 2.37

ground relative to other piles and its verticality are both kept within tolerable limits.

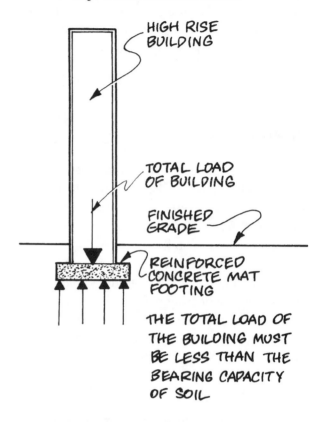

MAT FOOTING
USED FOR HEAVY LOADS AND
LOW BEARING SOIL CAPACITY

Figure 2.38

Piles may be made of wood, steel, concrete, or a composite of two materials. The choice of pile material depends primarily on the size of the load and the presence of moisture, with its potential for deterioration. Concrete piles are generally most suitable under all conditions, particularly where permanence is a factor.

Piles are driven into the earth by steam, air, or diesel hammers that drop from one to four feet. Piles may also be jetted into place with high-pressure water jets, but this method, because of the danger of overexcavating, is rarely advised. In driving a pile, care must be taken with respect to position, alignment, and possible drift, so that its predetermined location in the

The safe carrying capacity of a pile can be determined by pile-driving formulas, static pile formulas, or pile load tests, which are the most dependable.

Another type of deep foundation is a vertical shaft drilled into the ground and then filled with concrete. If it transmits its load to the soil by skin friction, it often is called a *drilled pile*. If it transfers the load by end bearing, it is called a *drilled caisson*. Frequently the bottom of the shaft is enlarged, or belled, to form a larger bearing area. Drilled piles and caissons sometimes require a steel casing, which is removed as the concrete is poured.

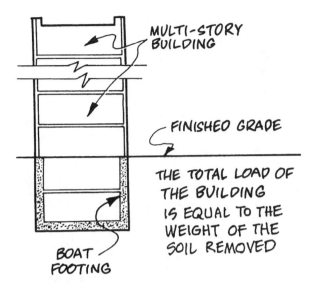

BOAT FOOTING
USED IN AREAS OF LOW
BEARING SOIL CAPACITY

Figure 2.39

Caissons and Cofferdams

Box-like structures used where very wet or soft soils are encountered are also called caissons. They provide a method of constructing foundations below water level, and may be formed from timber; steel (sheet piling); or concrete. Excavation is performed within the

caisson. For bridge piers or similar construction located in water, the entire area is surrounded with watertight sheet piling, the water is pumped out, and the foundations are then constructed. Such an installation is known as a cofferdam.

TEMPORARY SUPPORTS

During the construction of a foundation, it is often necessary to provide temporary support, or shoring, for excavated earth or existing structures. This is commonly achieved by means of sheeting, bracing, and/or underpinning.

Sheeting is a temporary wall of wood, steel, or precast concrete to retain the soil around an excavation.

A *slurry wall* is a type of sheeting in which a narrow trench is filled with a slurry, or soupy mixture, of bentonite clay and water, which resists the pressure of the earth. After the trench excavation is completed, reinforcing steel is lowered into the trench, concrete is placed from the bottom up, and the slurry is pumped out.

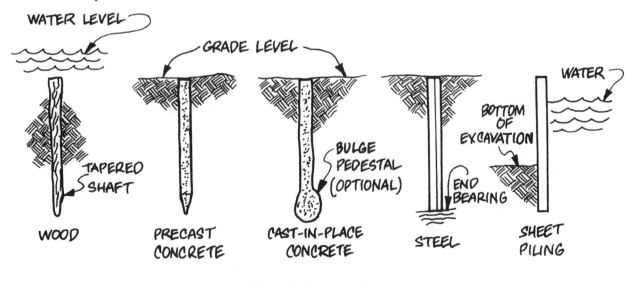

TYPES OF PILING

Figure 2.40

The site is now excavated, and the reinforced concrete wall is tied back as the excavation progresses to resist the earth pressure.

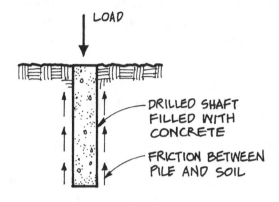

DRILLED PILE

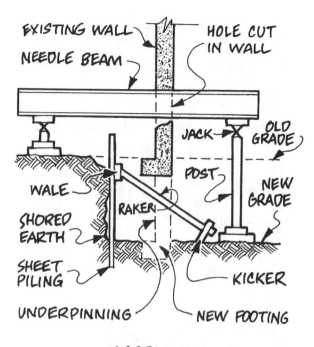

NEEDLING

Figure 2.42

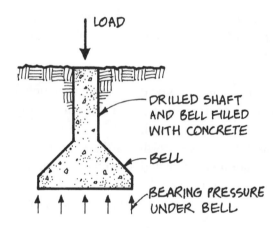

DRILLED & BELLED CAISSON

Figure 2.41

Bracing is used to brace the sheeting to resist the soil pressure. One common method is the use of diagonal braces called *rakers*.

However, rakers interfere with the excavation process. Therefore, where soil conditions permit, tiebacks into the surrounding soil or rock can be used in place of rakers, thus keeping the excavation clear and more accessible.

PILING CHART	
Type of Pile	**Remarks**
1. Wood	Must be below permanent ground water level
2. Precast concrete	Round, square, or octagonal, often prestressed
3. Cast-in-place concrete	Driven with mandrel core, removed before pouring
4. Concrete-filled steel pipe	Driven with sealed tip, then filled with concrete
5. Structural steel	For dense earth and heavy loads — H section
6. Sheet piling	May be used as a water dam

Table 2.4

Underpinning is employed to support existing foundations or walls being extended downward to the level of a new, deeper foundation. The two most common methods of underpinning involve *needle beams* or pipe cylinders with hydraulic jacks.

SITE IMPROVEMENTS

Site work invariably involves many kinds of improvements that are not part of the structure. These include roads and walks, fences, walls, lighting, and other such common landscape features. Roads and parking areas are most frequently constructed from concrete, or from asphalt, which is discussed below.

Asphalt Paving

Asphalt paving is a term that encompasses several bituminous paving products, all of which derive from asphaltic petroleum. Asphalt is applied, either hot or cold, in a single layer over a prepared foundation. A sub-base course of crushed stone or gravel is covered by a base course of finer aggregate. After rolling and tamping, the final asphalt surface is applied, two to three inches in thickness, depending on the amount of wear expected. The surface drainage of asphalt paved surfaces is critical, for even the slightest depression will result in unsightly and harmful ponding of water. Following are several types of asphalt paving in common use:

Asphaltic concrete consists of asphalt cement and graded aggregates, proportioned and mixed in a plant, transported to the site, spread over a firm foundation, and rolled while still hot.

Cold laid asphalt is the same as asphaltic concrete, except cold liquid asphalt and aggregates are used.

Asphalt macadam begins with a base of crushed stone, gravel, or slag compacted to a smooth surface. It is then sprayed with asphalt emulsion or hot asphalt cement in controlled quantities, covered with fine aggregate, and finally rolled until the smaller aggregate fills the voids in the coarse aggregate.

Other Paving Materials

Paving materials other than concrete or asphalt are used principally for pedestrian walks and may include brick, stone cobbles, granite setts, and flagstones.

Brick paving is a very popular and durable surface for pedestrian traffic. The material can be laid over a sand or cement/sand bed, but it is far more permanent when laid on a concrete slab foundation. Smooth bricks or bricks that are often wet may become slippery underfoot; this disadvantage, however, may be overcome to some extent with proper drainage.

Stone cobbles are mainly used for decorative effect. The best cobbles are rounded riverbed stones, from two to four inches in diameter, that are closely set in cement mortar. Cobbles can be set in a variety of patterns or in a random fashion.

Granite setts are small, rectangular or square blocks of granite that are set in a cement mortar to produce a very durable paved surface. Many years ago, city streets were often paved in this manner, but due to their high cost, granite setts are used today only in small areas and mainly for decorative purposes.

Flagstones refer to thin slabs of slate, bluestone, or soapstone. They are available with various surface textures, rough to smooth, and in various colors. Flagstones are installed over a sand bed or with mortar on a concrete slab.

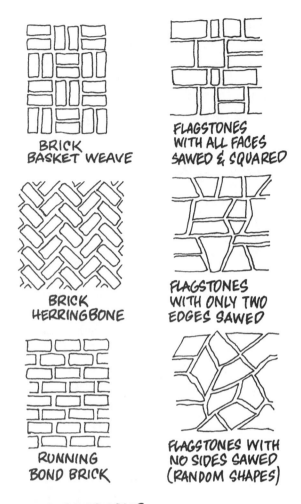

PAVING PATTERNS

Figure 2.43

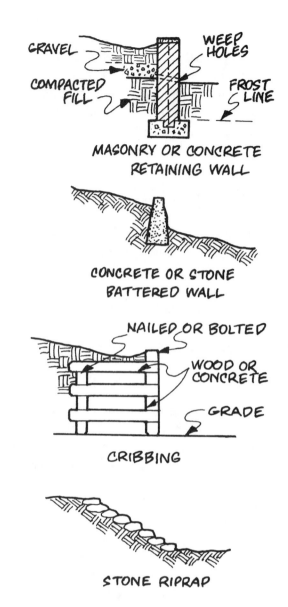

METHODS TO ACCOMMODATE VERTICAL
GRADE CHANGES
Figure 2.44

Grade Changing Devices

Grade changing devices are the means by
which earth is shaped or retained in order to
modify the finish grade of a site. The most
obvious device, of course, is a concrete or
masonry retaining wall. In addition, however,
there are other devices in common use, some of
which are illustrated in Figure 2.44.

LANDSCAPING

Landscaping completes, links, and harmo-
nizes the connections between buildings, open
spaces, natural features, and human beings.
Manmade landscapes, if they are to achieve
this goal, demand clarity of purpose and artistic

skill. The landscape designer combines earth, rock, water, plants, and other details to develop open spaces to their maximum potential.

In contrast to architectural space, site space is larger, and looser in form. It is generally a passive space, intended for exterior circulation, recreation, and quiet enjoyment. Much of it has no assigned usage, other than complementary relief. The landscape designer must consider climate, light, weather, orientation, scale, and the activities that are to take place on the site. Bright light sharpens or emphasizes details. Shadows define surfaces. Twilight creates unifying composition. Weather changes the appearance of an outdoor space considerably.

The character and visual effects of exterior spaces are quite different from those of interior space. In a building, a room 15 feet square may feel quite comfortable, while an outdoor space of the same size may feel very small.

In addition to the earth, rock, and water, the landscape designer employs trees, shrubs, ground cover, and plants. One of the tasks of a landscape architect is the locating of shrubs and trees. Although there are many landscape designs in which natural vegetation plays a role, there are also many great urban plazas that are devoid of vegetation. Nevertheless, plants are one of the fundamental landscape materials for site enhancement.

Because trees and plants require many years to mature, the planner must exercise great care in preserving existing vegetation. Natural amenities may be needlessly destroyed by insensitive and expedient grading.

Unfortunately, planting is often the first item to be eliminated when budget problems appear. Much care should be taken, therefore, to retain existing plants and trees in the total landscape plan.

CONIFEROUS

WINTER   SUMMER
DECIDUOUS

Figure 2.45

In the selection and placement of plants, the designer must consider such criteria as suitability, visual effect, future growth patterns, spacing, and overall pattern. Plant species should be able to endure the wear of anticipated traffic. They should be chosen with regard to maintenance requirements. Within these constraints, the designer may choose from a large range of plants, suitable, of course, to the environment.

Plant materials can be used effectively in landscaping to reduce the effects of climate extremes. Vegetation filters the rays of the sun. It can control the extent of heat radiated from the ground through the use of ground cover. Trees and shrubbery can block solar radiation. Vegetation can also reduce the effects of wind by obstruction, filtration, or deflection. Plant material may ameliorate the impact of precipitation. It can affect the rate of evaporation of moisture from the ground.

Control of the effects of solar radiation, wind, precipitation, and humidity contributes to human comfort during the day and at night.

The effectiveness of various plants in reducing the extremes of climate depends on their form and character. Indigenous plant materials provide the designer with numerous choices of vegetation to influence the climate within the project area.

Vegetation may absorb as much as 90 percent of the light energy which falls upon it. It can reduce wind speed to less than 10 percent. It can reduce daytime temperatures by as much as 15°F.

The visual characteristics of various plants offer a wide choice for the designer. Plants may be coarse or fine in texture. They may be dense or loose in leaf structure, smooth or rough, dull or shiny. Plants may grow vertically or horizontally. Their shape can be angular, rounded, or cylindrical.

In selecting plant materials, the designer must consider the potential hardiness, form, structure, foliage, flower, fruit, and amount of care that will be required for their maintenance. Plants can be arranged to form enclosures or shelters, provide screens or windbreaks, or offer shade. The designer must be familiar with the plants that best serve each purpose. The form, texture, color, and density of a plant determine the ability of the plant, or the group of plants, to serve as a design element. This enables a designer to utilize plants for space articulation, screening, shading, and privacy control.

Comprehensive landscape design involves the use of various materials for paved areas, steps, and walls. It involves the design of sculptured forms and objects, foundations and pools,

illumination and signage, seating and planters. There are many materials available for use as paving, including stone, brick, concrete, and asphalt. Each material has a different appearance as well as durability. Selection must consider cost, durability, and aesthetic qualities. Thought must also be given to the relationship between materials.

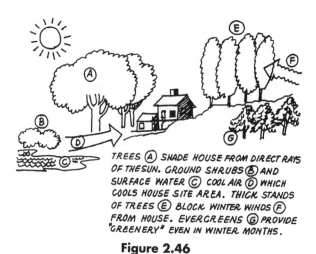

TREES (A) SHADE HOUSE FROM DIRECT RAYS OF THE SUN. GROUND SHRUBS (B) AND SURFACE WATER (C) COOL AIR (D) WHICH COOLS HOUSE SITE AREA. THICK STANDS OF TREES (E) BLOCK WINTER WINDS (F) FROM HOUSE. EVERGREENS (G) PROVIDE "GREENERY" EVEN IN WINTER MONTHS.

Figure 2.46

Intelligent planting and landscape design can reduce the effects of climate in the following ways:

1. Trees may be used to screen winds.
2. Conifers are more suited for the control of winter winds than deciduous trees.
3. Trees can be used to direct wind flow, and to increase ventilation in desired areas.
4. Vegetation, particularly needle-leafed trees, capture moisture, reduce fog, and thus increase the amount of sunlight reaching the ground.
5. Deciduous trees screen out direct sunlight in the summer while allowing it to pass in the winter.
6. Planted areas are cooler during hot days and have less heat loss during the night.
7. Indigenous vegetation is usually less costly, has a higher survival rate, and will require less maintenance.

SITE DEVELOPMENT COSTS

Introduction

An architect usually strives to produce the best architectural solution for the least amount of money. Consequently, decisions made during the design phase must consider not only the project's aesthetic qualities, but also its initial expense and maintenance cost throughout its useful life. To be successful, the architect must evaluate alternative site development schemes, select an optimum solution, estimate various options, and compare costs and their impact on the total budget of a project. He or she must be familiar with materials, systems, and construction operations.

For example, an architect must be able to analyze slope and soil conditions and evaluate alternative building sites in order to recommend an optimum location for structures that minimizes the cost of earthwork, footings, and soil preparation for landscaping. Or the architect

may have to review the costs of various methods of surfacing or illuminating roads and walkways and select the most cost-effective system available. This does not imply that the least expensive is always the preferred solution. The selection of site materials and systems must result in the appropriate solution that serves the owner's functional needs in the most economical manner. Consequently, the architect must evaluate and prioritize materials and systems and select those that are most responsive to the specific needs of the program.

Scope, Quality, and Cost

The design of a site, no matter how large or small, is affected by the scope of its development, the quality of the work, and the limitations imposed by the project's budget. An owner may establish the scope of the work based on anticipated needs, express a preference for a certain quality of materials and workmanship, and establish a total budget for the project. In such cases, the architect must

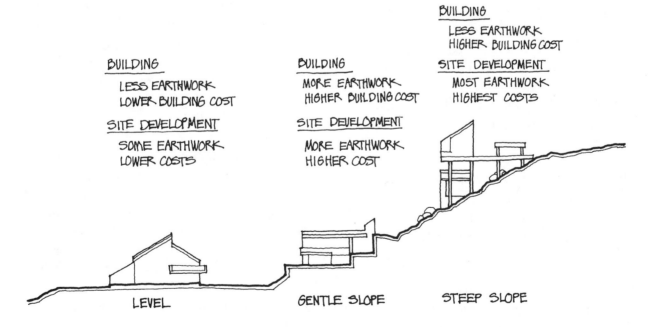

COMPARATIVE BUILDING AND SITE DEVELOPMENT COSTS

Figure 2.47

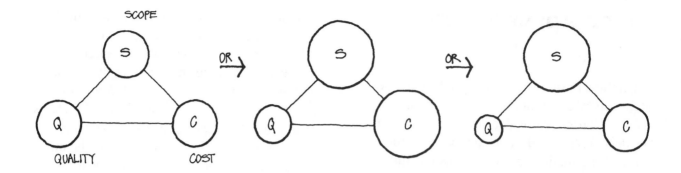

SCOPE , QUALITY , AND COST

Figure 2.48

retain the right to determine the affordable level of quality in order to assure the project's successful completion within the established budget.

For example, if the cost estimate exceeds the budget because the owner wishes to use brick paving, and he or she is unwilling to reduce the quantity or increase the amount budgeted for paved walkways, the architect must insist on a reduction in quality of the paving material. He or she may suggest a compromise solution that utilizes a combination of paving brick and concrete to retain some of the desired quality and appearance without exceeding the budgeted cost.

Under no circumstances should all three aspects—scope, quality, and cost—be fixed: one or two must always remain variable. For example, if both scope and quality are rigidly defined in the program, then the budget must remain flexible. If the estimated costs exceed the budget, the architect must evaluate both scope and quality and recommend viable alternatives for the owner's consideration. This may imply, in the case of paved walks, for example,

either reducing the total area of paving or selecting a less costly material, or both.

Although the initial installation cost is more apparent during the development of a project, maintenance costs may have a greater impact on the total cost over the life of the project. This requires estimating the initial cost and the cost to maintain or replace the material or system over a period of time, and comparing one system against another. An example of this is the selection of a more expensive material such as brick, requiring no finish, instead of concrete, which may have to be painted initially as well as periodically.

Because construction costs are always changing and vary considerably from one part of the country to another, it is unlikely that exam candidates will be required to know specific costs related to site work, or to prepare cost estimates for a given scope of site development work. Nevertheless, a candidate may have to demonstrate the ability to compare relative costs of various materials and systems, as well as their long range cost benefits. Aspects of site work will, most likely, include some of the following:

1. Demolition of existing buildings, site improvements, and natural features such as trees, rock outcroppings, etc., to make room for new developments

2. Earthwork, including cut, fill, compaction, etc., to prepare a site for buildings, roads, and other improvements

3. Foundations, considering the effect of soil conditions and topography on the cost of footings

4. Utilities, including the installation of new services as well as the extension of existing lines to provide the necessary services to a site

5. Paved roads and walkways

6. Landscaping

7. Lighting to illuminate roads, walks, paved areas, parking areas, and recreational areas

8. Site furniture, including benches or other seating, plant containers, and sports equipment

Initial Costs

Site construction costs are influenced by the cost of labor and materials, the efficiency of the contractor in managing the construction project, and the technology utilized to accomplish the work. Two important factors that affect site development costs are the characteristics of the site and the design of its development.

Unfavorable site conditions, such as a high water table, problems of access, poor soils, or steep slopes may result in excessive site development costs.

Careful attention in relating structures to topography, existing utilities, and vegetation, and the selection of materials and finishes, may exert an even greater impact on site development costs. Consequently, the architect must be aware of the comparative cost of the various elements comprising site work in order to select the optimum materials or systems, compatible with the overall project quality and budget.

Extensive earthwork, paving, storm drainage, or utility extensions increase construction costs, often requiring the deletion of landscaping or other site amenities so as not to exceed the project's total development budget. Consequently, if economical design were the principal consideration in planning a proposed project, what basic standards would the designer apply in selecting an appropriate site? He or she would recommend a site that is neither steeply sloping nor completely flat; a site with good natural soil, capable of supporting normal building loads, free of organic material, uncompacted fill, or rock within a few feet of the surface; and a site that has favorable natural drainage. The site would have a regular geometric shape and be served by the required utilities located close to its property lines.

In making preliminary recommendations, the architect would suggest a compact grouping of buildings so that connecting roads and walks could be kept to a minimum. Connecting elements would be arranged in a regular pattern that avoids useless leftover spaces, and have simple geometric shapes. Common areas would be compact, regularly shaped, and concentrated in a central location, rather than spread out over the site. Landscaping would be limited to grass, in order to control dust; paved surfaces would be asphaltic concrete for roads and walks; and there would be very few, if any, retaining walls, raised planters, seating units, or other site amenities.

Fortunately, however, many owners do not insist on a "bare bones" project budget. Rather, they encourage the architect to incorporate site improvements that enhance the environment, and to select materials and systems that create an aesthetically pleasing, low-maintenance, well-balanced design.

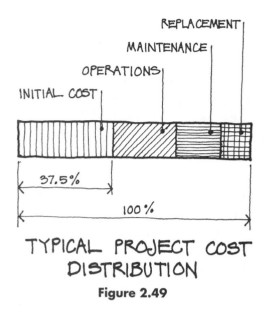

TYPICAL PROJECT COST DISTRIBUTION
Figure 2.49

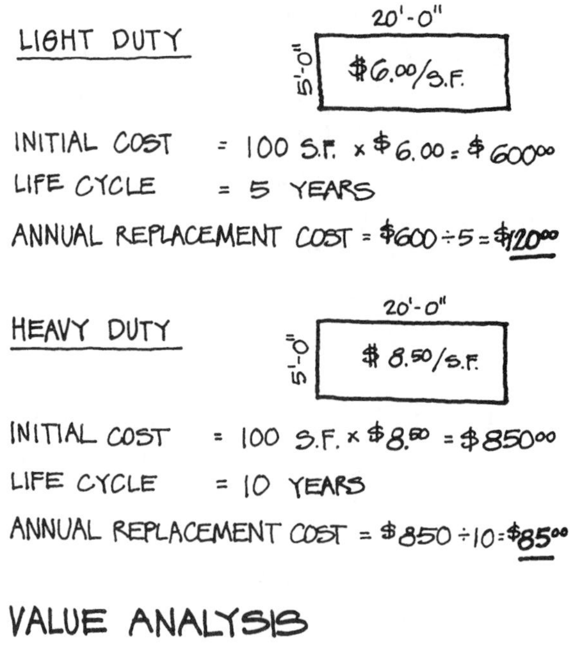

LIGHT DUTY   20'-0"   5'-0" $6.00/S.F.

INITIAL COST = 100 S.F. × $6.00 = $600.00
LIFE CYCLE = 5 YEARS
ANNUAL REPLACEMENT COST = $600 ÷ 5 = $120.00

HEAVY DUTY   20'-0"   5'-0" $8.50/S.F.

INITIAL COST = 100 S.F. × $8.50 = $850.00
LIFE CYCLE = 10 YEARS
ANNUAL REPLACEMENT COST = $850 ÷ 10 = $85.00

VALUE ANALYSIS
Figure 2.50

Long Range Costs

Evaluating alternative materials and systems must include a comparison of maintenance costs as well as initial installation costs, because the latter represent only a fraction of the entire cost of a project over the period of its useful life. Value analysis is a systematic method of obtaining optimum value for every dollar spent, considering all project expenditures, including construction, maintenance, operation, and replacement. Although value analysis is not commonly applied to site work, the designer attempts to employ similar principles in order to obtain maximum value for the client's money, both initially and over the life of the project. The performance of a material or system over a period of years may be as important to an owner as its initial cost. For example, a durable paving material may be more appropriate where heavy use is anticipated than less expensive paving, which must be resurfaced at more frequent intervals. Heavy duty paving for roads may cost 50 percent more than light duty asphalt paving; however, if it lasts twice as long before requiring replacement, it will be 25 percent more cost effective for each life cycle of the material.

Since construction costs continually escalate, it is unlikely that candidates will be required to know unit costs for specific elements of site work. More likely, the exam will concentrate on comparative costs, cost benefits, and the candidate's ability to select the most appropriate material or system for a given set of circumstances.

For example, the installation of a poured concrete paving slab over buried utility lines that require frequent maintenance is less cost effective than placing these utilities in a concrete trench with removable concrete covers, even though the latter is considerably more expensive initially.

Cost Control

To keep site development costs to a minimum, the designer must consider various alternatives in developing a design concept. The major elements comprising site development work and means to control their economic impact on projects are listed below. Cost-effective design utilizes a logical approach to siting buildings and other improvements, resulting in an efficient physical organization of the site. The following examples illustrate that point.

1. Locate buildings along gently sloping terrain; avoid steeply sloping land. Why? To minimize costs of grading and excavation for building footings, retaining walls, roads, and utility lines. For example, locate a development of attached multi-family dwellings in a cluster along gentle slopes, somewhat above the base of the hill, rather than near its steeply sloping crest, in order to avoid excessive earthwork, unconventional building footings, and steeply sloping utility runs, and to provide ease of access.

2. Locate buildings where positive natural drainage exists. Why? To avoid redirecting surface flow by excessive regrading of the land and/or installing expensive storm drainage systems to dispose of storm water. For example, don't locate buildings and other site improvements at the base of a natural drainage basin, where rapid runoff of rain water requires costly methods of interception to avoid flooding.

3. Arrange vehicular circulation systems on the site to follow contours rather than to oppose them. Why? To minimize the cost of earthwork, construction of banks, berms, and retaining walls. For example, a two-mile long road following the existing contours will require considerably less excavation and associated sitework than a half-mile road up one side of the mountain and down the other, even though the former requires four times the amount of surface preparation and paving.

4. Locate paved parking lots on relatively level ground, rather than sloping ground. Why? To avoid excessive reshaping of the land, terracing, steps, and ramps to connect the various levels, and complex storm drainage systems to avoid standing water on paved surfaces. For example, a parking lot required to accommodate a large number of cars located on a sloping site must be constructed in small, terraced segments connected by ramps for vehicles and steps for pedestrians. This requires more paving, curbs, and gutters, complex drainage devices, and more site lighting, all contributing to increased development costs.

5. Locate buildings so they relate to new and existing utility systems. Why? To minimize the length of connecting runs of utility lines. For example, a close physical relationship between utilities and buildings minimizes excavation, trenching, and service runs. Amenities requiring few or no utilities, such as tennis courts, may be located farther from utilities.

6. Locate site improvements to utilize existing vegetation. Why? To avoid the removal of trees and plants and their replacement with costly new landscaping. For example, take advantage of the shading characteristics of mature deciduous trees by placing buildings north of them, rather than demolishing and removing them, grubbing, and grading the vacated area and preparing the site for new construction requiring new trees.

7. Avoid locating improvements over rock, organic soil, or areas of high water table. Why? To minimize costly excavation and foundation problems. For example, locating buildings where granite or limestone occurs close to the surface requires blasting prior to normal excavation, thereby increasing foundation costs considerably.

8. Coordinate the location of new with existing facilities including buildings, roads, walks, and other improvements in the development of a site design concept. Why? To preclude unnecessary and costly

demolition and replacement of existing improvements. For example, try to utilize existing roads, utilities, etc., in the design of a new or expanded site development. Should demolition costs be included in the project development budget? Yes!

9. Select appropriate finish materials for site improvements, including paving of roads, walks, plazas, play courts, etc., retaining walls, planter walls, seating and other site furniture. Why? To provide finished surfaces that best serve the specific function of the site and are in balance with the overall level of quality for the particular project, building type, and its anticipated life. For example, select broom-finished concrete in preference to slate or granite for campus walks, malls, and steps, to provide a useful, durable, easily maintained finish, appropriately priced for most construction budgets of educational facilities. (Note: Granite steps at the State Capitol, however, might very well be preferred.)

10. Select indigenous plant material for landscaping. Why? To minimize maintenance, irrigation, and replacement costs. For example, drought-tolerant plants (xerophytes) are preferred over water-loving plants (hydrophytes) in arid climates, where water is scarce and irrigation costly. Plants unaccustomed to a hostile climate will inevitably have to be replaced more frequently than indigenous species.

11. Select site lighting systems in consideration of capital cost, energy cost, and replacement lamp and labor cost. Why? To effect cost savings in the installation, operation, and maintenance of site lighting systems. For example, select high pressure sodium or metal halide lamps in preference to incandescent lamps for parking lot lighting, for lower energy consumption, ease of maintenance, and longer life.

ZONING

General

The first American zoning ordinance was enacted in New York City in 1916 to limit the size and shape of new skyscrapers so that the adjacent streets would not become permanently shaded canyons. Most zoning statutes in the 1920s dealt with physical development. They divided cities into districts of different uses, with uniform regulations for each. For example, residential districts permitted only residences, commercial districts only commercial activities, and so on. Major categories were further divided; for example, industry was divided into heavy manufacturing and light manufacturing. Residential use was divided into single-family, two-family, and multiple-family dwellings. Homogeneous districts were based on the idea that differing uses within a district would lower property values. Multi-use districts, sometimes called *cumulative zoning*, allowed residences in commercial zones and residential and commercial uses in industrial zones.

The ordinances of the 1920s also regulated the height and bulk of buildings and setback lines. The intent of these acts was to allow the owner to develop the land as he or she wished, as long as the specific restrictions of the ordinances were not violated. These laws authorized, but did not compel, local authorities to control development decisions. They did not offer incentives to owners to undertake desirable development, but rather, attempted to avoid undesirable development.

Since that time, the ordinances have changed considerably; instead of prohibiting poor planning, they now encourage, and sometimes even compel, desirable planning.

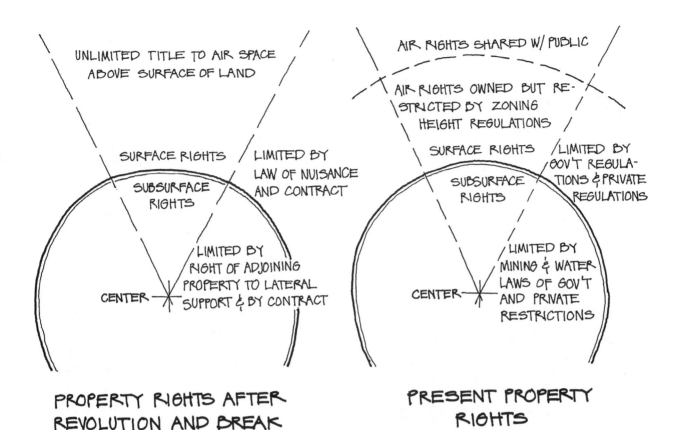

UNLIMITED TITLE TO AIR SPACE ABOVE SURFACE OF LAND

SURFACE RIGHTS / LIMITED BY LAW OF NUISANCE AND CONTRACT

SUBSURFACE RIGHTS

CENTER — LIMITED BY RIGHT OF ADJOINING PROPERTY TO LATERAL SUPPORT & BY CONTRACT

PROPERTY RIGHTS AFTER REVOLUTION AND BREAK FROM ENGLAND

AIR RIGHTS SHARED W/ PUBLIC

AIR RIGHTS OWNED BUT RE- STRICTED BY ZONING HEIGHT REGULATIONS

SURFACE RIGHTS / LIMITED BY GOV'T REGULA- TIONS & PRIVATE REGULATIONS

SUBSURFACE RIGHTS

CENTER — LIMITED BY MINING & WATER LAWS OF GOV'T AND PRIVATE RESTRICTIONS

PRESENT PROPERTY RIGHTS

Figure 2.51

SHADED URBAN CANYONS

Figure 2.52

The enactment of the Model Land Development Code recognized aesthetics, environmental problems, and the preservation of historical sites as planning and development factors. In New York City, developers commonly add plazas at the ground level of office towers, in return for permission to erect taller buildings. For example, IBM was allowed to build five additional floors in return for creating a tree-filled atrium at the foot of its Madison Avenue building.

Zoning ordinances often restrict the height and size of buildings, as well as their location on the site. They may prescribe setbacks from property lines, limit percentage coverage of the lot area, restrict the number of dwellings per acre (density), and require a specific amount of off-street parking, as well as numerous other possible regulations.

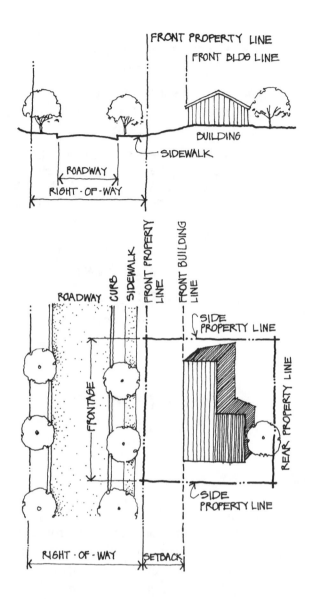

TYPICAL DEVELOPMENT STANDARDS
Figure 2.53

Zoning Envelope

The volume within which a building may be placed is sometimes referred to as the *zoning envelope*. This is an imaginary, tent-like space inside of which the building may be placed in any location, so long as it does not penetrate any of the imaginary surfaces. Figure 2.54 depicts a highly simplified zoning envelope. Most of these have more complex shapes determined by several interacting standards and restrictions.

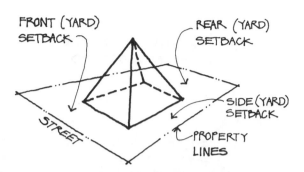

THE ZONING ENVELOPE
Figure 2.54

Setbacks and Yards

A zoning ordinance often regulates the distance between a street and a building, as well as between buildings. The main purposes of such restrictions are to provide building interiors with natural light and ventilation, inhibit the spread of fire from one structure to the next, and minimize conflicts between street traffic and off-street activities. These ordinances also allow for future street widening and create space open from the ground to the sky. The regulations for yards and other setbacks establish the base of the zoning envelope (the ground area within which construction may occur). The drawing above shows a lot for a single-family house and the various yards referred to in zoning ordinances.

A setback is the horizontal space adjacent to a property line into which a structure may not project. Setbacks provide a sense of openness, as well as light and air. They may also be required for off-street parking, or they may be primarily for aesthetic reasons. In some instances, setbacks are established as a function of the building's height using a formula which requires taller buildings to be further back from property lines, in order to assure a minimum amount of openness to the sky. Most ordinances allow paved parking areas within setbacks; however, they may require trees at specific intervals or low walls at property lines in order to screen the rows of parked automobiles.

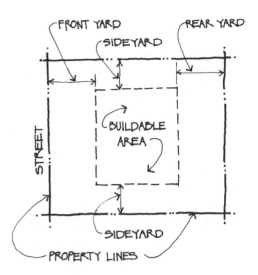

TYPICAL YARDS
SINGLE FAMILY DISTRICT
Figure 2.55

Height Limitations and Variable Setbacks

Zoning ordinances may limit the number of stories in a building, its height in feet above street level, or both. The height is usually measured from grade, which may be defined in various ways, depending on the local zoning ordinance. For example, grade may be defined as the lowest adjacent ground elevation, the average adjacent ground elevation, or perhaps some other elevation. Thus, the way in which grade is defined may affect the number of stories permitted, particularly on a sloping site.

Some zoning ordinances contain variable height and setback requirements, either in place of absolute limits, or in addition to them. For example, in Figure 2.56, no portion of a building may be placed closer to the street than an imaginary plane inclined at an angle of 60 degrees with the street and extending upward from the center line of the street. A control of this sort encourages a "ziggurat" building profile.

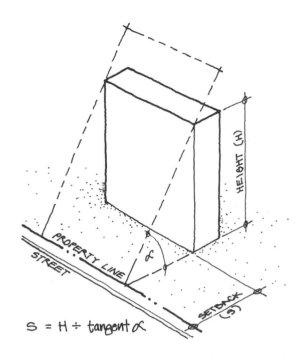

$$S = H \div \tan \alpha$$

SETBACK AS
A FUNCTION OF HEIGHT
Figure 2.56

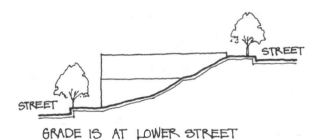

GRADE IS AT LOWER STREET

GRADE IS AT HIGHER STREET

ALTERNATE INTERPETATION
OF GRADE
Figure 2.57

Height limitations are more common in residential zones than in commercial or industrial zones. Crowded urban areas, such as New York City, limit the number of stories in order to control the population density and the resulting traffic, and to retain a certain amount of sky exposure.

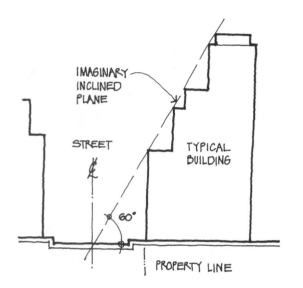

SETBACK BASED ON INCLINED PLANE

Figure 2.58

Land Coverage

In addition to the basic zoning envelope, there are other restrictions which determine how large a building may be placed on a site. These controls, which involve the amount of development, limit the proportion of the site that may be covered by buildings (land coverage) and the ratio of total usable floor space to total site area (floor area ratio or FAR). Land coverage is expressed as a maximum percentage of total available land area that may be covered by a building or buildings. The open land may be used for surface developments, such as parking, plazas, recreation and other types of landscaped spaces, and level or depressed courtyards. The purpose of these restrictions is to encourage the retention and development of open spaces, to enhance the environment through the admittance of light and air, and to provide planted areas to relieve the hard surfaces of buildings, sidewalks, and streets.

Floor Area Ratios

The floor area ratio (FAR) is the ratio of the floor area of a building to the total area of the site. The purpose of an FAR ordinance is to

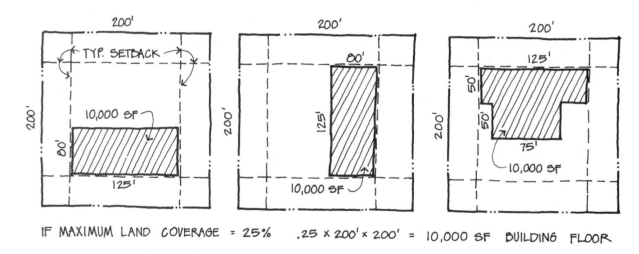

THREE OPTIONS FOR LAND COVERAGE

Figure 2.59

control the amount of site development and to restrict the bulk of a building, in order to encourage openness, light, and air, especially in urban areas.

Thus, a floor area ratio of 2.0 would permit 40,000 square feet of floor space on a site of 20,000 square feet (2 × 20,000). A ratio of 2.5 would permit 50,000 square feet of floor space on the same site. The drawings in Figure 2.60 show three options that would be available to the owner of a lot having a maximum FAR of 4. In each of the three illustrations, the lot size is the same: 100,000 square feet. Thus in each case, the maximum floor area allowed is 400,000 square feet. In figure A, the owner has covered the entire site with a four-story structure containing 100,000 square feet per floor. In figure B, half of the site has been covered. Since each floor has 50,000 square feet, the building can be eight stories. In figure C, the entire site is covered with a one-story structure,

using up 100,000 of the 400,000 square feet of floor area allowed, and the remaining 300,000 square feet have been put into a 12-story tower, with each level containing 25,000 square feet of usable floor area.

In all of these examples, floor area may be either the net usable space, excluding stairs, elevators, and other similar spaces, or the total gross area of the building, depending on the ordinance.

Off-Street Requirements

Many cities require an owner to provide a minimum number of off-street parking spaces for a building's tenants and visitors. For residential buildings these requirements are usually expressed in terms of parking spaces per dwelling unit. If dwellings are small, one space may be required; for larger units, however, two spaces are normally a minimum. For office

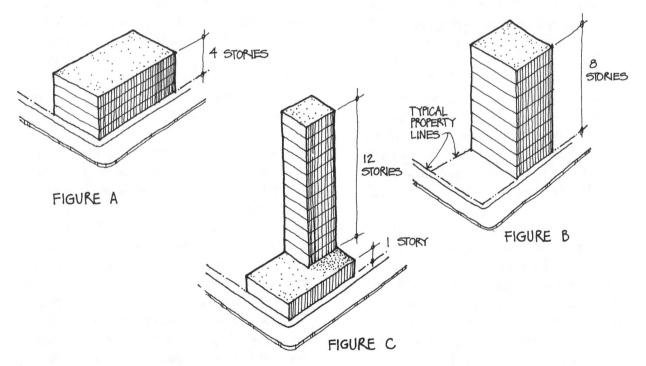

THREE OPTIONS WHERE FLOOR·AREA·RATIO IS 4.0/LOT IS 100,000 SF.

Figure 2.60

buildings in commercial zones, the requirement is usually stated as one space for a specified amount of usable floor area. For example, if the requirement is one parking space for every 500 square feet of usable floor area and the building contains 50,000 square feet, the owner must provide parking facilities for no less than 100 cars (50,000 ÷ 500) within the limits of his or her property. In some cases where space is limited, it may be possible to satisfy the parking requirement on a separate site, provided it is located within a prescribed distance from the building site. Some districts also require a certain amount of site area for loading and unloading of service vehicles, particularly in the case of hospitals, hotels, and institutions.

FLEXIBLE ZONING

General

The purpose of flexible zoning is to overcome the rigidity of traditional zoning and to make the regulations relevant to changing patterns of development. Most zoning ordinances continue to reflect the basic principles of the traditional ordinances of the 1920s: regulations which rigidly define the way land may be used and limitations concerning its physical development. More recently, certain modifications have been introduced which make zoning ordinances more flexible, while preserving their intent.

The *conditional use*, for example, is a departure from traditional zoning, which prohibited any uses in a district other than those specifically allowed by the ordinance. Other significant deviations from traditional zoning concepts include the *planned unit development* (cluster concept), the *floating zone*, *incentive (bonus) zoning*, and *contract zoning*. Together, these devices are sometimes called *flexible zoning*.

Variances and Conditional Uses

Because even the best zoning ordinances may cause an unintentional hardship to owners of specific land parcels, most cities have established boards which have the authority to grant exceptions to or deviations from the precise terms of these ordinances. These exceptions are called *variances*. Theoretically, a variance is granted when the literal application of an ordinance would cause an undue hardship in the proposed development of a site. For example, a site may have a width of 280 feet in an area where the zoning ordinance specifies the minimum to be 300 feet; however, the site exceeds the minimum lot size by 20 percent. Under these circumstances, a zoning board might grant a variance reducing the lot width requirement because the property conforms generally to the intent of the law.

Conversely, if all existing buildings along one side of a street are set back 20 feet from the front property line, a zoning board would be reluctant to grant a variance allowing an owner to build up to the property line, because this would create a detrimental visual contrast, easily perceived by the surrounding property owners and the public.

The purpose of a *conditional use* in a zoning ordinance is to provide for flexibility within a district. If a use is described in an ordinance as a "conditional use," it is permitted only if specified conditions are met, a public hearing has been held, and approval has been given by the local governing body. A conditional use is normally granted if it is considered to be in the public interest. A school serving local residents, for example, may be permitted in a residential zone, providing it conforms to certain criteria for traffic, pedestrian walks and crosswalks, and noise control. Under such circumstances

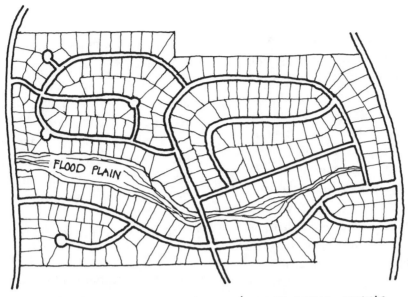

CONVENTIONAL DEVELOPMENT / TRADITIONAL ZONING

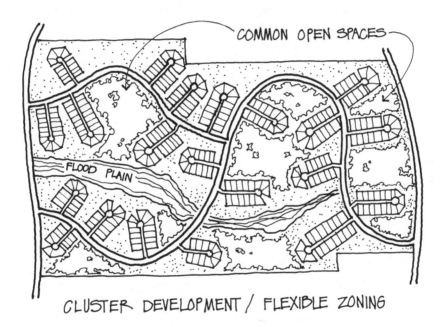

CLUSTER DEVELOPMENT / FLEXIBLE ZONING

FLEXIBLE ZONING

Figure 2.61

a zoning board may grant the conditional use of a site subject to restrictions for the protection of adjacent property owners. The granting of a conditional use or special-use permit does not, however, change the zoning of the particular parcel of land. If the development is abandoned, the conditional use would no longer apply and the property would revert to its original district designation.

Rezoning

The only alternative available to a landowner who cannot meet the requirements for a conditional use permit is to seek rezoning of his or her property. Rezoning, however, can cause hardships to neighboring property owners. Under the strict interpretation of a zoning ordinance, a choice may have to be made between the interests of the landowner and those of the neighboring property owners. Rezoning small individual lots results in *spot zoning*, which may alleviate an owner's hardships. There are times, however, when rezoning is accomplished through political manipulation, rather than for legitimate reasons. For example, rezoning a parcel of property from residential to commercial might appear to have a reasonable basis, while the real reason may be to increase the value of the property for the benefit of its owner.

Contract Zoning

An agreement between a developer and local government to restrict usage or height, or to provide additional setbacks or buffers, over and above what is required by the ordinance, in return for certain benefits, is called contract zoning. For example, a developer may agree to additional restrictions in return for being granted approval of a conditional use. Such restrictions exceed the requirements of the local ordinance and are legally binding.

Contract zoning gives the local governing body power to rezone land or issue special permits granting permission to develop land for nonconforming uses in exchange for a developer's commitment to perform certain compensating acts. In San Francisco, for example, a developer must pay for the construction or renovation of a certain number of housing units whenever he or she plans to erect a new office building. The purpose is to create new dwellings for office workers in an already crowded area with housing shortages. Should the developer balk, he or she must contribute a certain amount of money to a housing bond program, based on the area of new office construction. Other promised acts or conditions might include noise abatement, traffic control, or the erection of walls and landscaped buffer zones. As an alternative, the developer may be allowed to contribute the necessary funds to the local authority in lieu of performing the work himself.

Bonus or Incentive Zoning

Traditional zoning is inflexible in the sense that owners are forbidden to develop their property contrary to the zoning ordinance. Traditional zoning, therefore, prevents the worst from happening, but that is all it can do. It cannot assure good planning since it is only a restraint. Architects have opposed the negative aspects of zoning while searching for ways to make it a more positive force in development. Gradually, ordinances have been modified in order to reward builders for benefiting communities.

In some cities, zoning requirements may be waived if the developer provides bonus features, as in the IBM Building in New York. This is often attractive to the developer, because not only can the floor area or height of a building be increased, for example, but the bonus features may provide amenities which make the project more desirable for tenants, thereby increasing rents.

Incentives can be given for a variety of reasons: street widenings, providing unobstructed views (as along a shore line), inclusion of theaters and retail space in office buildings, provision of walkways for public use (such as a pedestrian bridge over a street), and preservation of open space. Since open space is the most common objective of incentive zoning, allowing a greater floor area ratio is probably the most prevalent incentive. For example, the developers of the Bankers Trust Building in Manhattan were allowed greater tower height and floor area in exchange for providing a large elevated open plaza and a two-level covered arcade of shops.

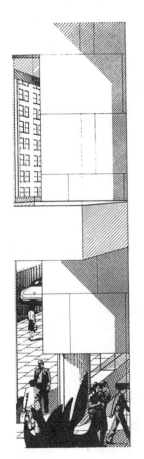

INCENTIVE ZONING :
A STREET - LEVEL ART GALLERY
IN EXCHANGE FOR A LARGER F.A.R.

Figure 2.62

LESSON 2 QUIZ

1. Which of the following will most effectively divert subsurface water away from a building's foundation?

   A. Place the foundation below the water table

   B. Modify the contours of the site during finish grading

   C. Install drainage tiles adjacent to the bottom of footings

   D. Provide a bed of coarse gravel at the perimeter of the foundation

2. If the loads of a proposed structure are high relative to the bearing capacity of the soil, one would likely provide

   A. a mat footing.

   B. continuous wall footings.

   C. combined footings.

   D. shallow spread footings.

3. A system of piles may be appropriate for supporting a structure when

   A. moisture in the soil is detected.

   B. the piles can be placed below ground water level.

   C. dense earth makes conventional excavation difficult.

   D. the surface soil has low bearing capacity.

4. Frost line refers to the level of earth

   A. at which the soil bearing value is affected by weather.

   B. at which the building foundation should be located.

   C. below which the footings will not freeze.

   D. below which the soil does not freeze.

5. For a structure with very heavy loads resting on dense earth, which of the following would be most appropriate?

   A. Boat footings

   B. Jetted piles

   C. Wood piles

   D. Structural steel piles

6. Placing load on a footing results in

   A. reduced soil bearing capacity.

   B. differential settlement.

   C. a reduction of the soil's void volume.

   D. shrinkage of the soil.

7. The principal purpose of all soil exploration and testing is to determine the

   A. bearing capacity of the soil.

   B. intrinsic character of the soil.

   C. depth of the water table.

   D. depth of the bedrock.

8. The design of a surface drainage system for a residential development is based on a five-year storm. During a review, the drainage system is found to be incapable of handling the expected runoff. Therefore, it should be

   A. changed to a subsurface system.

   B. changed to employ non-erosive materials.

   C. designed for a 10-year storm.

   D. designed for a 100-year storm.

9. In the residential development of the previous question, runoff might be reduced by using

   A. flat roofs, rather than sloped roofs, on the residential units.

   B. wider roof eaves on the residential units.

   C. more paved areas.

   D. greater areas of vegetation.

10. All of the following describe the general climatic characteristics of an area, EXCEPT

    A. temperature.

    B. topography.

    C. humidity.

    D. wind velocity.

SUSTAINABLE DESIGN

by Jonathan Boyer, AIA

INTRODUCTION

Architects can no longer assume that buildings function independently of the environment in which they are placed. In the late 1800s the machine age offered the lure of buildings that were self-sufficient and independent of their natural surroundings—"The Machine for Living," as LeCorbusier proclaimed.

In the middle of the 20th century, the promise of endless and inexpensive nuclear energy lured architects into temporarily ignoring the reality of the natural elements affecting architectural design. Why worry about natural systems if energy was going to be infinite and inexpensive? Glass houses proliferated.

Energy is not free, the global climate is changing, and the viability of natural ecosystems is diminishing. Architects are designing structures that affect all these natural ecosystems. Much as Marcus Vitruvius wrote thousands of years ago that architects must be sensitive to the local environment, architects are returning to study the virtues of tuning to natural systems. Contemporary architects must combine their knowledge of the benefits of natural systems with the understanding of the selective virtues of contemporary innovative technologies.

This lesson focuses on the fundamental principles of environmental design that have evolved over the thousands of years that humans have been creating spatial solutions.

HISTORY OF SUSTAINABLE DESIGN

In early human history, builders of human habitats used materials that occurred naturally in the earth, such as stone, wood, mud, adobe bricks, and grasses. With nomadic tribes and early civilizations, the built environment made little impact on the balance of natural elements. When abandoned, the grass roof, adobe brick, or timber beam would slowly disintegrate and return to the natural ecosystem. Small human populations and the use of natural materials had very little impact on a balanced natural ecosystem.

But as human populations expanded and settlements moved into more demanding climates, natural materials were altered to become more durable and less natural. In fact, archeological finds demonstrate some of the human creations that are not easily recycled into the earth; fired clay, smelted ore for jewelry, and tools are examples of designs that will not easily reintegrate into the natural ecosystem. These materials may be reprocessed (by grinding, melting, or reworking) into other human creations, but they will never be natural materials again.

As human populations expanded, there is strong evidence that some civilizations outgrew their natural ecosystem. When overused, land became less fertile and less able to support crops, timber, and domesticated animals necessary for human life. The ancient solution was to move to a more desirable location and use new natural resources in the new location, abandoning the ecologically ruined home site.

The realization that global natural resources are limited is an age-old concept. The term *conservation,* which came into existence in the late 19th century, referred to the economic management of natural resources such as fish, timber, topsoil, minerals, and game. In the United States, at the beginning of the 20th century, President Theodore Roosevelt and his chief forester, Gifford Pinchot, introduced the concept of conservation as a philosophy of natural resource management. The impetus of this movement created several pieces of natural legislation to promote conservation and increased appreciation of America's natural resources and monuments.

In the middle of the 1960s, Rachel Carson published *Silent Spring,* a literary alarm that revealed the reality of an emerging ecological disaster—the gross misunderstanding of the value and hazards of pesticides. The pesticide DDT and its impact on the entire natural ecosystem was dramatic; clearly, some human inventions were destructive and could spread harm throughout the ecosystem with alarming speed and virulence. Birds in North America died from DDT used to control malaria in Africa. Human creations were influenced by the necessities of the natural cycles of the ecosystem. Human toxic efforts could no longer be absorbed by the cycles of nature. Human activities became so pervasive and potentially intrusive that there needed to be a higher level of worldwide ecological understanding of the risk of disrupting the ecosystem.

Architects, as designers of the built environment, realize the ecological impact of their choices of architectural components, such as site selection, landscaping, infrastructure, building materials, and mechanical systems. The philosophy of sustainable design encourages a new, more environmentally sensitive approach to architectural design and construction.

There are many credos for the approach to a new sustainable design. Some architectural historians maintain that the best architects (Vitruvius, Ruskin, Wright, Alexander) have always discussed design in terms of empathy with nature and the natural systems. Now it is evident that all architects should include the principles of sustainable design as part of their palette of architectural best practices.

PRINCIPLES OF SUSTAINABLE DESIGN

The tenets outlined below indicate why it is necessary to maintain the delicate balance of natural ecosystems.

1. In the earth's ecosystem (the area of the earth's crust and atmosphere approximately five miles high and five miles deep) there is a finite amount of natural resources. People have become dependent on elements such

as fresh water, timber, plants, soil, and ore, which are processed into necessary pieces of the human environment.

2. Given the laws of thermodynamics, energy cannot be created or destroyed. The resources that have been allotted to manage existence are contained in the ecosystem.

3. All forms of energy tends to seek equilibrium and therefore disperse. For example, water falls from the sky, settles on plants, and then percolates into the soil to reach the subterranean aquifer. Toxic liquids, released by humans and exposed to the soil, will equally disperse and eventually reach the same underground reservoir. The fresh water aquifer, now contaminated, is no longer a useful natural resource.

There is a need to focus on the preservation of beneficial natural elements and diminish or extinguish natural resources contaminated with toxins and destructive human practices.

There are many credos for environmental responsibility. One, *The Natural Step,* was organized by scientists, designers, and environmentalists in 1996. They were concerned with the preservation of the thin layer that supports human life in a small zone on the earth's surface: the ecosphere (five miles of the earth's crust) and the biosphere (five miles into the troposphere of the atmosphere).

Their principles are as summarized as follows:

1. Substance from the earth's crust must not systemically increase in the ecosphere.

   Elements from the earth such as fossil fuel, ores, timber, etc., must not be extracted from the earth at a greater rate than they can be replenished.

2. Substances that are manufactured must not systemically increase in the ecosphere.

Manufactured materials cannot be produced at a faster rate than they can be integrated back into nature.

3. The productivity and diversity of nature must not be systemically diminished.

This means that people must protect and preserve the variety of living organisms that now exist.

4. In recognition of the first three conditions, there must be a fair and efficient use of resources to meet human needs.

This means that human needs must be met in the most environmentally sensitive way possible.

5. Buildings consume at least 40 percent of the world's energy. Thus they account for about a third of the world's emissions of heat-trapping carbon dioxide from fossil fuel burning, and two-fifths of acid rain-causing carbon dioxide and nitrogen oxides.*

The built environment has a monumental impact on the use of materials and fuels to create shelter for human beings. The decisions about the amount and type of materials and systems that are employed in the building process have an enormous impact on the future use of natural resources. Architects can affect and guide those decisions of design to influence the needs of sustainability and environmental sensitivity.

---

*   Sources: David Malin Roodman and Nicholas Lessen, "Building Revolution: How Ecology and Health Concerns are Transforming Construction." Worldwatch Paper 124 (Washington DC, Worldwatch Institute, 1995); Sandra Mendler & William Odell, The HOK Guidebook to Sustainable Design, (New York: John Wiley & Sons, Inc., 2000).

SUSTAINABLE SITE PLANNING AND DESIGN

Most architectural projects involve the understanding of the design within the context of the larger scale neighborhood, community, or urban area in which the project is placed.

If the building will be influenced by sustainable design principles, its context and site should be equally sensitive to environmental planning principles.

Sustainable design encourages a re-examination of the principles of planning to include a more environmentally sensitive approach. Whether it is called Smart Grow, sustainable design, or environmentally sensitive development practice, these planning approaches have several principles in common.

Site Selection

The selection of a site is influenced by many factors including cost, adjacency to utilities, transportation, building type, zoning, and neighborhood compatibility. In addition to these factors, there are sustainable design standards that should be added to the matrix of site selection decisions:

■ **Adjacency to public transportation**
If possible, projects that allow residents or employees access to public transportation are preferred. Allowing the building occupants the option of traveling by public transit may decrease the parking requirements, increase the pool of potential employees and remove the stress and expense of commuting by car.

■ **Floodplains**
In general, local and national governments hope to remove buildings from the level of the 100-year floodplain. This can be accomplished by either raising the building

at least one foot above the 100-year elevation or locating the project entirely out of the 100-year floodplain.

This approach reduces the possibility of damage from flood waters, and possible damage to downstream structures hit by the overfilled capacity of the floodplain.

- **Erosion, fire, and landslides**
  Some ecosystems are naturally prone to fire and erosion cycles. Areas such as high slope, chaparral ecologies are prone to fires and mud slides. Building in such zones is hazardous and damaging to the ecosystem and should be avoided.

- **Sites with high slope or agricultural use**
  Sites with high slopes are difficult building sites and may disturb ecosystems, which may lead to erosion and topsoil loss. Similarly, sites with fertile topsoil conditions—prime agricultural sites— should be preserved for crops, wildlife, and plant material, not building development.

- **Solar orientation, wind patterns**
  Orienting the building with the long axis generally east west and fenestration primarily facing south may have a strong impact on solar harvesting potential. In addition, protecting the building with earth forms and tree lines may reduce the heat loss in the winter and diminish summer heat gain.

- **Landscape site conditions**
  The location of dense, coniferous trees on the elevation against the prevailing wind (usually west or northwest) may decrease heat loss due to infiltration and wind chill factor. Sites with deciduous shade trees can reduce summer solar gain if positioned properly on the south and west elevations of the buildings.

Alternative Transportation

Sites that are near facilities that allow several transportation options should be encouraged. Alternate transportation includes public transportation (trains, buses, and vans); bicycling amenities (bike paths, shelters, ramps, and overpasses); carpool opportunities that may also connect with mass transit; and provisions for alternate, more environmentally sensitive fuel options such as electricity or hydrogen.

Reduction of Site Disturbance

Site selection should conserve natural areas, and restore wildlife habitat and ecologically damaged areas. In some areas of the United States, less than 2 percent of the original vegetation remains. Natural areas provide a visual and physical barrier between high activity zones. Additionally, these natural areas are aesthetic and psychological refuges for humans and wildlife.

Storm Water Management

There are several ways by which reduced disruption of natural water courses (rivers, streams and natural drainage swales) may be achieved:

- Provide on-site infiltration of contaminants (especially petrochemicals) from entering the main waterways. Drainage designs that use swales filled with wetland vegetation is a natural filtration technique especially useful in parking and large grass areas.

- Reduce impermeable surface and allow local aquifer recharge instead of runoff to waterways.

- Encourage groundwater recharge.

Ecologically Sensitive Landscaping

The selection of indigenous plant material, contouring the land, and proper positioning of shade trees may have a positive effect on the landscape appearance, maintenance cost, and ecological balance. The following are some basic sustainable landscape techniques:

- Install indigenous plant material, which is usually less expensive, to ensure durability (being originally intended for that climate) and lower maintenance (usually less watering and fertilizer).

- Locate shade trees and plants over dark surfaces to reduce the "heat island effect" of surfaces (such as parking lots, cars, walkways) that will otherwise absorb direct solar radiation and retransmit it to the atmosphere.

- Replace lawns with natural grasses. Lawns require heavy maintenance including watering, fertilizer, and mowing. Sustainable design encourages indigenous plant material that is aesthetically compelling but far less ecologically disruptive.

- In dry climates, encourage xeriscaping (plant materials adapted to dry and desert climates); encourage higher efficiency irrigation technologies including drip irrigation, rainwater recapture, and gray water reuse. High efficiency irrigation uses less water because it supplies water directly to the plant's root areas.

Reduction of Light Pollution

Lighting of site conditions, either the buildings or landscaping, should not transgress the property and not shine into the atmosphere. Such practice is wasteful and irritating to the inhabitants of surrounding properties. All site lighting should be directed downward to avoid "light pollution."

Open Space Preservation

The quality of residential and commercial life benefits from opportunities to recreate and experience open-space areas. These parks,

wildlife refuges, easements, bike paths, wetlands, or play lots are amenities that are necessary for any development.

In addition to the aforementioned water management principles, the following are principles of design and planning that will help increase open-space preservation:

- **Promote in-fill development** that is compact and contiguous to existing infrastructure and public transportation opportunities.

  In-fill development may take advantage of already disturbed land without impinging on existing natural and agricultural land.

  In certain cases, in-fill or redevelopment may take advantage of existing rather than new infrastructure.

- **Promote development that protects natural resources** and provides buffers between natural and intensive use areas.

  First, the natural areas (wetlands, wildlife habitats, water bodies, or floodplains) in the community in which the design is planned should be identified.

  Second, the architect and planners should provide a design that protects and enhances the natural areas. The areas may be used partly for recreation, parks, natural habitats, and environmental education.

  Third, the design should provide natural buffers (such as woodlands and grasslands) between sensitive natural areas and areas of intense use (factories, commercial districts, housing). These buffers may offer visual, olfactory, and auditory protection between areas of differing intensity.

  Fourth, linkages should be provided between natural areas. Isolated islands of natural open space violate habitat boundaries and make the natural zones seem like captive preserves rather than a restoration or preservation of natural conditions.

Fifth, the links between natural areas may be used for walking, hiking, or biking, but should be constructed of permeable and biodegradable material. In addition, the links may augment natural systems such as water flow and drainage, habitat migration patterns, or floodplain conditions.

■ **Establish procedures that ensure the ongoing management of the natural areas** as part of a strategy of sustainable development.

Without human intervention, natural lands are completely sustainable. Cycles of growth and change including destruction by fire, wind, or flood have been occurring for millions of years. The plants and wildlife have adapted to these cycles to create a balanced ecosystem.

Human intervention has changed the balance of the ecosystem. With the relatively recent introduction of nearby human activities, the natural cycle of an ecosystem's growth, destruction, and rebirth is not possible.

Human settlement will not tolerate a fire that destroys thousands of acres only to liberate plant material that reblooms into another natural cycle.

The coexistence of human and natural ecosystems demands a different approach to design. This is the essence of sustainable design practices, a new approach that understands and reflects the needs of both natural and human communities.

AHWAHNEE PRINCIPLES

In 1991, in the Ahwahnee Hotel in Yosemite National Park, a group of architects, planners, and community leaders met to present community principles that express new, sustainable planning ideas. These principles are summarized below.

Preamble

Existing patterns of urban and suburban development seriously impair our quality of life. The symptoms are: more congestion and air pollution resulting from our increased dependence on automobiles, the loss of precious open space, the need for costly improvements to roads and public services, the inequitable distribution of economic resources, and the loss of a sense of community. By drawing upon the best from the past and the present, we can plan communities that will more successfully serve the needs of those who live and work within them. Such planning should adhere to certain fundamental principles.

Community Principles

1. All planning should be in the form of complete and integrated communities containing housing, shops, workplaces, schools, parks, and civic facilities, essential to the daily life of the residents.

2. Community size should be designed so that housing, jobs, daily needs, and other activities are within easy walking distance of each other.

3. As many activities as possible should be located within easy walking distance of transit stops.

4. A community should contain a diversity of housing types to enable citizens from a wide range of economic levels and age groups to live within its boundaries.

5. Businesses within the community should provide a range of job types for the community's residents.

6. The location and character of the community should be consistent with a larger transit network.

7. The community should have a center focus that combines commercial, civic, cultural, and recreational uses.

8. The community should contain an ample supply of specialized open space in the form of squares, greens, and parks, whose frequent use is encouraged through placement and design.

9. Public spaces should be designed to encourage the attention and presence of people at all hours of the day and night.

10. Each community or cluster of communities should have a well-defined edge, such as agricultural greenbelts or wildlife corridors, permanently protected from development.

11. Streets, pedestrian paths, and bike paths should contribute to a system of fully connected and interesting routes to all destinations. Their design should encourage pedestrian and bicycle use by being small and spatially defined by buildings, trees, and lighting, and by discouraging high speed traffic.

12. Wherever possible, the natural terrain, drainage, and vegetation of the community should be preserved with superior examples contained within parks or greenbelts.

13. The community design should help conserve resources and minimize waste.

14. Communities should provide for the efficient use of water through the use of natural drainage, drought tolerant landscaping, and recycling.

15. The street orientation, the placement of buildings, and the use of shading should contribute to the energy efficiency of the community.

Regional Principles

1. The regional land-use planning structure should be integrated within a larger transportation network built around transit rather than freeways.

2. Regions should be bounded by and provide a continuous system of greenbelt/wildlife corridors to be determined by natural conditions.

3. Regional institutions and services (government, stadiums, museums, and so forth) should be located in the urban core.

4. Materials and methods of construction should be specific to the region, exhibiting a continuity of history and culture and compatibility with the climate to encourage the development of local character and community identity.

Implementation Principles

1. The general plan should be updated to incorporate the above principles.

2. Rather than allowing developer-initiated, piecemeal development, local governments should take charge of the planning process. General plans should designate where new growth, in-fill, or redevelopment will be allowed to occur.

3. Prior to any development, a specific plan should be prepared based on these planning principles.

4. Plans should be developed through an open process and participants in the process should be provided visual models of all planning principles.

Source: Local Government Commission's Center for Livable Communities, http://lgc.org/clc/.

USGBC—U.S. GREEN BUILDING COUNCIL

Incorporated as a nonprofit trade association in 1993, the U.S. Green Building Council (USGBC) was founded with a mission "to promote buildings that are environmentally responsible, profitable and healthy places to live and work." It is formed of leaders from across the building industry who head a national consensus for producing a new generation of buildings that deliver high performance inside and out.

The core of the USGBC's work is the creation of the Leadership in Energy and Environmental Design (LEED) green building rating system. LEED provides a complete framework for assessing building performance and meeting sustainability goals. Based on well-founded scientific standards, LEED emphasizes state of the art strategies for sustainable site development, water savings, energy efficiency, materials selection, and indoor environmental quality. LEED recognizes achievements and promotes expertise in green building through a comprehensive system offering project certification, professional accreditation, training, and practical resources.

USGBC committees are actively collaborating on new and existing LEED standards, including a standard for homes, neighborhood development, and commercial interiors.

Their Web site is: *www.usgbc.org.*

ARCHITECTURAL PROCESS

After the planning process has been concluded, and the site has been selected, the architectural team will begin to focus on the project, including the project's buildings and related infrastructure.

Traditionally, the architect is faced with four components to every design decision: cost, function, aesthetics, and time. The new paradigm adds *sustainability* to this list.

The ingredients of the normal process have been discussed previously, but the new ingredient, sustainability, changes the meaning of all these pieces of the architectural process.

Cost

As architects put together budgets for their clients, they are always concerned with the first costs of the design components—the initial cost to purchase and install the design element.

Sustainable design has made the economic decision process more holistic. The decision to select a design element (such as a window, door, flooring, exterior cladding, or mechanical system) is now concerned with the "life cycle" cost of the design.

Life-Cycle Costing

Life-cycle costing is concerned not only with the first cost, but the operating, maintenance, periodic replacement, and residual value of the design element.

For example, two light fixtures (A and B) might have different first cost: Fixture A has a 10 percent more expensive first cost than B. But when the cost of operation (the lamps use far less energy per lumen output) and the cost of replacement (the bulbs of A last 50 percent longer than the bulbs of Fixture B) is evaluated, Fixture A has a far better life-cycle cost and should be selected.

In this kind of comparison, the life-cycle cost may be persuasive; the extra cost of Fixture A may be recovered in less than two years due to more efficient operation and replacement savings. In this situation the architect justified Fixture A to the owner, who benefits from a more energy efficient lighting that continues to save the owner operating costs for the life of the building.

Matrix Costing

While designing a typical project, the architect faces numerous alternate decisions, a process that may be both intriguing and complex.

Sustainable design adds an ingredient to the matrix of decisions that may actually help the composition.

For example, decisions that allow the improved efficiency of the building envelope, light fixtures, and equipment may permit the architect to allow the engineer to reduce the size of the HVAC system, resulting in a budgetary trade-off. The extra cost of the improved envelope may be economically balanced by the diminished cost of the mechanical system.

This type of economic analysis, which evaluates cost elements in a broad matrix of interaction, is a very valuable architectural skill. The ability to understand the interaction between different building systems in a creative and organized fashion can differentiate an excellent from a simply adequate architectural design.

Function

Functionality is one of the primary standards of architectural design. If the building does not perform according to the client's needs, then the building design has failed.

Years ago, the design element could perform at the highest level regardless of its impact on the environment or energy use. The fact that many industrial and residential buildings are operat-

ing in 2003 much more efficiently than 1960 is evidence that the building design and construction profession is learning how to tune buildings to a higher degree of energy operation. But, with diminishing natural resources and increasing pollution of the environment, even more efficient design is necessary.

Today, architects will include sustainability in the selection of optimal functional design components.

For example, a roof system must be able to withstand a variety of weather conditions, be warranted to be durable a minimum of years, be able to be applied in a range of weather conditions, and have a surface with reflectivity that does not add to the urban heat effect.

Time

The schedule of a project is always a difficult part of the reality of the design process. Time is a constraint that forces a systematic and progressive evaluation of the design components.

The sustainable component of the architectural process may add to the amount of time the architect will spend on the research for the project.

The architect may spend more time on a sustainable design with the result being a more integrated, sustainable project.

Aesthetics

The aesthetic of a project is the combination of the artistry of the architect and the requirements of the project.

Sustainable design has the reputation of emphasizing function and cost over beauty and appeal.

It is the architect's responsibility to keep all the design tools in balance. A project without aesthetic consideration will fail the client, its user, and the potential client who may be deciding between the normal design and one that considers a broader, integrated, sustainable approach.

Sustainability

The fifth point is a new component that leads to a new approach to the design process.

Sustainable designs should have five goals:

1. Use less
2. Recycle components
3. Use easily recycled components
4. Use fully biodegradable components
5. Do not deplete natural resources necessary for the health of future generations

STANDARDS FOR EVALUATION

How can we objectively evaluate the quality of a sustainable project?

The architect is faced with responding to many standards and regulations in the course of assembling a design. Building codes, life safety standards, fire code, zoning regulations, and health and sanitary regulations are some of the many municipal, state, and federal standards that an architect must evaluate in the course of any project.

Sustainability is a new filter for the design process and there are several organizations that have offered checklists for evaluating the inclusion of environmentally sensitive elements into the project.

One of the measures of performance is LEED (Leadership in Energy & Environmental Design), which is sponsored by the USGBC (U.S. Green Building Council). This standard was developed in the 1990s by a consortium of building owners, architects, suppliers, engineers, contractors, and governmental agencies.

The goal of LEED and similar environmental design standards is to introduce new sustainable approaches and technologies to the construction industry. LEED is a voluntary environmental rating system that is organized into six categories:

1. Sustainable sites
2. Water efficiency
3. Energy and atmosphere
4. Materials and resources
5. Indoor air quality
6. Innovation and design practice

LEED covers the range of architectural decisions, including site design, water usage, energy conservation and production, indoor air quality, building materials, natural lighting, views of the outdoors, and innovative design components.

The LEED point award matrix is a mixture of teaching, persuasion, example, and incentive. It is good checklist for the entire project team to evaluate the quality of sustainable design decisions for the complete project—from initial planning through final construction, maintenance, and training procedures.

These categories combine *prerequisites* (basic sustainable practices such as building commissioning, plans for erosion control, or meeting minimum indoor air quality standards) with optional *credits* (water use reduction, heat island reduction, or measures of material recycled content).

Most of the credits are performance based—solutions based on system performances against an established standard such as American Society of Heating, Refrigeration and Air Conditioning Engineers (ASHRAE). ASHRAE has created one of most widely recognized standards of energy design that is used by mechanical engineers and architects.

For example, one credit (under the Energy and Resources category) is "Optimize Energy Performance."

The number of points for this credit depend on how the architectural and engineering team can optimize the design of the building's energy systems against the ASHRAE 90.1 standards.

The possible design solutions include optimizing the heating, cooling, fans, pumps, water, and interior lighting systems.

In the graduated point matrix for a new building, if the team improves the performance (against ASHRAE standards) by 15 percent they receive one point and if they manage to improve by 60 percent they receive ten points.

LEED describes suggested results but allows the architectural team to find a variety of solutions. The LEED certification awards range from Bronze at 40 percent compliance to Platinum at 81 percent compliance. The LEED certification is innovative and rigorous, and currently there are fewer than a half dozen platinum buildings in the United States.

THE SUSTAINABLE DESIGN PROCESS

Is a sustainable design organized and implemented differently from a conventional design?

The Design Team

What kind of design team is necessary for a sustainable project?

The scope of a sustainable design invites an expanded team approach, which may include the following:

- Architects or engineers (structural, MEP) with energy modeling experience
- A landscape architect with a specialty in native plant material
- A commissioning expert (if LEED employed)
- An engineer/architect with building modeling experience

The design team for a sustainably designed project tends to have a larger pool of talent than a typical architectural project. Wetlands scientists, energy efficient lighting consultants, native plant experts, or commissioning engineers are examples of the additional talent that may be added to sustainable design projects.

As with any architectural design, there is a hierarchy of design goals:

- *Initial imperatives* such as budget, timing, image, and program necessities
- *Subjective goals* such as a functionally improved and more pleasing work environment, pleasing color schemes, and landscaping that complements the architecture
- *Specific goals* such as more open space, more natural light, less water usage, and adjacency to public transportation

And with the inclusion of sustainability there may be additional goals:

- *Initiatives that are specific to sustainability* such as fewer toxins brought into the space, daylighting in all spaces with people occupancies, less overall energy consumed, less water usage, adjacency to public transportation, and improved indoor air quality

■ Desire to exceed existing standards such as ASHRAE, USGBC, or American Planning Association (APA)

RESEARCH AND EDUCATION

Is additional education and research necessary for a sustainable project?

Yes. Innovative HVAC systems, durable yet nontoxic materials, recycled materials, recyclable materials, native plant material, energy efficient lighting, and controls are examples of design components that are not normally designed and installed by general contractors and architectural consultants on typical projects.

Education of the Client

Sustainable design requires a new way of examining the architectural design process. Concepts such as life-cycle costing, recycled versus recyclable materials; non-VOC (volatile organic compounds) substances; daylighting; and alternate energy sources are among the several new concepts that the architect should discuss with the client before the design process commences.

It is critical that the client understands the sustainable process and is sympathetic to its potential economic and environmental benefits.

Education of the Project Team

Once the project has been assigned to an architect, but before the design process begins, the project team (architect, engineer, contractor, consultants, and owner) should assemble and discuss the project scope and objectives with all the project team members.

Establishing Project Goals

Among the many items included in the scope of work (including the extent of work, program elements, budget, and schedule) are the objectives for sustainable design.

For example, the architect and owner might establish goals for several environmental areas such as:

■ X percent reduction of energy usage from the established norm (see "Benchmarking" later in this section)

■ Improved lighting (less energy used and more efficient dispersal of indirect light with less glare)

■ Nontoxic and low VOC paint and finishes

■ Increased recycled content in materials such as carpeting, gypsum wallboard, ceiling tiles, metal studs, and millwork

■ High-efficiency (energy star) appliances

■ Wood elements are all certified wood products

■ Daylighting in all work/occupied spaces

As the leader of the project team, it is the architect's responsibility to include sustainable goals with the rest of the project scope of work.

A detailed explanation of the benefits of these sustainable design elements to all of the project team will ensure that they fully understand the design potential and economic implications of these concepts.

Verify Extent of Work

Sustainable design involves a more comprehensive approach to pre-project planning.

The LEED certification process will require record keeping and verification of the source of materials—a process that is beyond the normal design and construction work. For purposes of selecting a contractor and consultants, the team should be briefed on these additional obligations.

For example, the demolition process (if LEED certified) will require verification that materials have been sorted and delivered to an approved recycling organization. By contrast, the normal demolition process does not require recycling or verification that each material is sorted by type.

Clearly establishing the extent and type of effort required for each member of the sustainable design team is critical. The extent and type of effort will affect each member's ability to participate and their fees for services and construction work.

Energy and Optimization Modeling

Building shape, orientation, fenestration location, roof color, envelope configuration, and HVAC system efficiency are some of the variables in sustainable design projects that can be fine tuned with DOE-2 (U.S. Department of Energy's building analysis program) and other computer energy modeling programs.

The "fine tuning" of a project's energy components is one of the elements in the architect's design matrix that affects the final appearance, cost, and performance of the final design.

Energy modeling will not govern the final design. Issues such as compatible scale, color, texture, and functionality are still part of the architect's palette. But energy modeling is one additional factor that the architect will employ as part of the "best practices" approach to architecture.

In addition, modeling can assist in the cost analysis of a project. The fact that the modeling program is interactive helps the architect simultaneously adjust design elements to demonstrate alternate energy efficient solutions.

For example, energy modeling might allow the architect to demonstrate to the team that a more durable, aesthetically pleasing, and energy efficient building skin could be economically justified by reducing the size and cost of the mechanical system.

The ability to visually and numerically quantify the efficacy of trading certain design elements may be an effective tool for the architect when discussing the building design with the consultants and owner.

The Bid and Specification Process

The requirements of a sustainable design will often vary from a normal project.

For example, the millwork section of bid documents will normally specify the finish material, configuration of the design and methods of attachment, delivery, and installation. But the requirement of non-VOC glues and non-VOC substrate may confuse a potential bidder and cause that bidder to increase the bid price unnecessarily.

To facilitate the bidding and construction process, the architect should include the following:

- Simple definitions of sustainable elements—for example, what "VOC," "certified" wood product, or "daylighting" mean
- Explanations of specific characteristics of sustainable elements—for example, specifically state the standard that must be met (for example, Green Label Testing

Program Limits, carpet's total VOC limit, that is, formaldehyde 0.05 (mg/m^2)

- References of specific regulatory agency's information (name, address, e-mail, phone, and so on)—for example, the Carpet and Rug Institute, *www.carpet-rup.com*, (800) 555-8846

- Examples of suppliers that could meet the sustainable standards indicated—in the case of sustainable products, there are at least two approaches to a list of suppliers for products:

  1. Limit the installer to three to five suppliers of a product that is known to satisfy the sustainable design specifications.

     This approach assures the architect that the product will meet specified standards.

     (Note, however, that with the constantly changing nature of the emerging sustainable design market, a limited list could limit competition and the diversity of creative alternatives.)

  2. Identify a list of qualified suppliers, but permit the bidder/contractor to submit alternative suppliers who satisfied the sustainable design criteria. This approach creates a more competitive environment, but it will require more effort of the architect to properly review and qualify the bids.

Changes and Substitutions

Every project is faced with the reality of time and budgetary pressures. And, in those instances, there may be situations when one product or design element may not be available in the form originally specified.

Sustainable designed projects require more stringent architectural supervision to ensure that original design standards are met.

For example, in the rush to project completion the installer may claim that paints used for "touch up" of damaged areas are so small that they may be installed with normal, higher-VOC paints. This minor transgression might jeopardize the integrity of the project and the ability to receive certification for LEED credits in certain areas.

ENERGY EVALUATION

In the climates of North America, buildings need some form of purchased energy (electricity, natural gas, oil) in order to operate. The architect works with his or her team to design strategies that may reduce the amount of purchased energy, reduce operating costs, and reduce the nation's dependence on imported fossil fuels.

The following are some design strategies that the sustainable design approach might employ to improve a building's energy performance. These elements are listed and briefly described.

Solar Design

Solar design is the age-old system of using sunlight or solar radiation to supply a portion of the building's heat energy. By a combination of techniques such as window and skylight design, location of internal thermal mass, and internal organization of the building's functions, solar design may replace some of the fossil fuel needed for heating and cooling buildings.

Passive solar systems is a category of solar design. Passive solar systems are those systems that permit solar radiation to fall on areas of the building that benefit from the seasonal energy conditions of the structure.

For example, some North American buildings are designed to reduce solar radiation gains from sunlight in the summer. Passive solar design relies on inherent qualities of the building's fenestration, massing, and orientation to capture sunlight.

Passive solar systems are usually categorized into direct or indirect gain systems.

Direct gain systems, as the title implies, are those systems that allow solar radiation to flow directly into the space needing heat. A process commonly known as the "greenhouse effect" allows much of the sunlight that passes through the glass of the fenestration to be retained in the material it strikes (stone, concrete, wood, etc.) inside the building. Thus, south facing windows allow solar radiation to be directly gained and used inside the building.

Indirect gain systems operate when the sunlight first strikes a thermal mass that is located between the sun and the space. The sunlight absorbed by the mass is converted to thermal energy (heat) and then transferred into the living space.

There are basically two types of indirect gain systems: thermal storage walls and roof ponds. The difference is essentially the location—roof verses wall materials.

Passive solar design might employ several architectural strategies to facilitate the design:

1. *Architectural sun control devices.* Overhangs or shading devices that have been designed to permit winter solar radiation from entering the building interior while blocking the higher angled, summer solar radiation from entering the building. Deciduous trees often perform the same function of permitting winter sunlight to enter and blocking much of the summer solar radiation with branches and leaves. Other examples include shutters; vertical projections or fins; awnings; trellises

(especially with shading vegetation); and sunscreens (some with PV panels that both gather sunlight to convert into electricity and shade unwanted radiation from interior space in the warm months).

2. *Light-colored roof systems.* Light-colored roofing materials reflect sunlight and reduce the amount of radiation that is absorbed through the roof into the interior space. Colors with higher reflectance (albedo) factors are preferred. For example, some cities in the United States require roof materials to have a minimum albedo rating of .65 (65 percent of the solar radiation is reflected back into the atmosphere). The urban heat island effect, caused by roofs, roads, and parking areas that absorb solar radiation during the day and retransmit the stored heat during the afternoon and evening, can be modified with light-colored roof systems.

    By designing these surfaces with light-colored and reflective material, the amount of heat energy stored in these materials is diminished and the urban heat island effect is reduced. Grass or vegetated roof areas have good insulating value and may also reduce the urban heat island effect and provide cooling through evapotranspiration.

3. *Optimized building glazing systems.* Orientation, light transmittance factors, and U-value are all factors architects consider in selecting glazing. Glass that is low-E (emissivity) is desirable because it is coated with a material that allows a maximum amount of sunlight to be transferred through the glass and not reflected back into the atmosphere.

Lighting

The illumination of the interior of a sustainably designed building requires a holistic approach that balances the use of artificial and natural lighting sources.

Daylighting

Properly filtered and controlled solar radiation may provide a valuable source of illumination to a building interior. This process is called "daylighting" (simply having properly designed fenestration that allows natural sunlight to replace or dramatically reduce the need for artificial lighting).

Because unwanted sunlight (particularly in summer months) can also add to the internal heat load of a building, the architect must be careful to allow only beneficial sunlight and reduce unwanted solar heat gain. There are several techniques for controlling daylighting:

Overhangs, fins, and other architectural shading devices

1. Sawtooth (not bubble) skylight design, which allows the glass to face north for illumination, not south for solar heat gain

2. Interior window shading devices, which allow solar gain during cool months, and the blocking of solar radiation during the warmer seasons

3. Light shelves, which permit the daylight to reflect off the ceiling and penetrate farther into the interior without affecting views outside

Higher Efficiency Light Fixtures

In addition to a daylighting strategy, light fixtures that are more efficiently designed reduce energy cost and increase comfort, such as the following:

- Fixtures that use fluorescent or HID lamps, which provide more illumination per watt than incandescent lighting.

- Fixtures that are designed to diffuse or bounce the illumination off the ceilings or internal reflectors, which are more efficient; cause less glare (especially in an environment with computer monitors); and save operating costs.

- Fixtures that have higher efficiency (T-8) fluorescent bulbs, which produce more lumens per watt and thereby diminish the heat generated by lighting.

- Fixtures that offer dimming or multiple switching capability, which permit the archi- tect a more energy efficient lighting design. Dimming or multiple switching fixtures allow the architect to design lighting patterns that blend nicely with daylighting opportunities. For example, an office with perimeter fenestration allows daylighting supplemented with overhead lighting that can be dimmed or reduced. The interior spaces, which are too far from the perimeter for daylighting, may be controlled with switches or dimmers that allow relatively higher levels of illumination. The result is an even illumination pattern, which saves on artificial lighting costs, by relying on daylighting at the perimeter.

- Fixtures that use higher efficiency lamps such as fluorescent, high intensity discharge (HID) sulfur lighting (exterior only).

- Fluorescent fixtures that use high efficiency electronic ballasts.

Additionally, the architect may avoid less efficient incandescent lighting where possible; install task lighting to supplement diffused ambient lighting; and install LED (light emitting diode) lighting for exit signs. LED lighting lasts longer than incandescent and is far less expensive to operate.

Lighting Sensors and Monitors

Where possible, lighting costs can be diminished by installing light monitors that sense occupancy conditions. As long as the room contains people, the lights will remain on. If people leave, the sensor will wait for a few minutes, then shut off all the lighting in the room.

Lighting sensors can be designed to operate with a preference for motion, heat (from people), or desired time of occupancy.

Lighting Models

Computer lighting models are one option that allows the architect to simulate the levels of sunlight that penetrate into a building design, depending on the building location, varying times of year, fenestration orientation, and design.

By incrementally altering fenestration (skylights, windows, or light transport systems) and the artificial lighting system, the architect may optimize the daylighting and artificial lighting systems for the building.

Benchmarking

The U.S. Department of Energy provides "benchmark" information of total energy consumption in BTUs/SF for various kinds of buildings in the United States. These standards, or benchmarks, can be useful in the measuring of energy efficiency standards for various types of buildings:

For example:

- Average for all office buildings (pre-1990)   104.2
- Average for all office buildings (1990–1992)   87.4
- Average for all educational buildings (pre-1900)   87.2
- Average for all educational buildings (1990–1992)   57.1
- Average for all laboratory buildings (pre-1990)   319.2
- Average for all health care buildings (pre-1990)   218.5

Source: U.S. Department of Energy, Commercial Building Energy Consumption and Expenditures.

Benchmarking is a good way to alert the design team to the base energy standards for their design. It's a good place to start and ultimately a standard to beat. And, one can see from some of the comparisons (office and educational buildings), that some energy efficiency is occurring.

COMMISSIONING

Commissioning is an organized process to ensure that all building systems perform interactively according to the intent of the architectural and engineering design, and the owner's operating needs.

Commissioning usually includes all HVAC and MEP systems, controls, ductworks and pipe insulation, renewable and alternate technologies, life safety systems, lighting controls and daylighting systems, and any thermal storage systems. Commissioning also verifies the proper operation of architectural elements such as the building envelope, vapor and infiltration control, and gaskets and sealant used to control water infiltration.

Commissioning is a process required for LEED certification, but is a recommended procedure for any building involved with sustainable design procedures.*

INNOVATIVE TECHNOLOGIES

Besides the aforementioned issues of solar design, improved lighting systems, improved HVAC systems, and improved building massing and envelope design, there are several "innova-

---

* *Source: Commissioning Requirements for LEED Green Building Rating, Version 8. February 5. 1999; Sandra Mendler and William Odell,* The HOK Guidebook to Sustainable Design, *New York, John Wiley & Sons, Inc.: 2000, p. 71.*

tive technologies" that the architect can offer to the project team for consideration.

Ground Water Aquifer Cooling and Heating (AETS)

One alternative to full air-conditioning with chillers, which make heavy demands on electricity, is the aquifer thermal energy storage, which uses the differential thermal energy in water from an underground well to cool a building during summer and heat a building in the winter.

This is an efficient, relatively low-cost system, but it may require approval from the local environmental authority before installation.

Geothermal Energy

Where appropriate, heat contained within the earth's surface causes macrogeological events (such as underground geothermal springs or lava formations) that may be tapped to produce heat for adjacent structures.

In select locations this heat energy can be transferred and conveyed to supplement a building's heating demand.

Wind Turbines

Small-scale wind machines used to generate electricity can be mounted on buildings or in open space nearby. These systems share several advantages:

- Relatively cost-effective
- Tested and established technology
- Systematic started-up
- Relatively high output

These systems share several disadvantages:

- Need a relatively high mast
- Require substantial structural support

- Present potential for noise pollution
- Visually intrusive

Photovoltaic (PV) Systems

The basis of the PV systems is the concept that electricity is produced from solar energy when photons or particles of light are absorbed by semiconductors.

Most PV systems are mounted to the building (either on the roof or as shading devices above fenestration). Currently, PV systems are not cost effective. But with promised government subsidy necessary to achieve an economy of scale, PVs may be a viable method of electrical production in the United States, Japan, and Germany in the near future.

Fuel Cells

Even though Sir William Grove invented the technology for the fuel cell in 1839, it has only recently been recognized as a potential power source for the future. The fuel cell claims to be the bridge between the hydrocarbon economy and the hydrogen-based society.

Fuel cells are electrochemical devices that generate direct current (DC) electricity similar to batteries. But, unlike batteries, they require a continual input of hydrogen-rich fuel. In essence, fuel cells are reactors that combine hydrogen and oxygen to produce electricity, heat, and water. They are clean, quiet, and emit no pollution when fed directly with hydrogen.

At the moment, fuel cell technology is still not cost effective for the commercial building market. Still, there seems to be a general feeling that hydrogen-based energy reactors will soon be an optional energy source.

Biogas

Biogas is produced through a process that converts biomass, such as rapid-rotation crops and selected farm and animal waste, to a gas that can fuel a gas turbine. This conversion process occurs through anaerobic digestion—the conversion of biomass to gas by organisms (like bacteria) in an oxygen-free environment.

Biogas has several advantages: it has relatively high energy production; it lends itself to both heat and power production; it creates almost zero carbon dioxide emissions; it virtually eliminates noxious odors and methane emissions; and it protects ground water and reduces the landfill burden.

Small-Scale Hydro

Harnessing the energy from moving water is one of the oldest energy production systems in the world. In some locations, small-scale hydro power is a efficient and clean source of energy and is devoid of environmental penalties associated with large scale hydro projects. It allows small scale, local energy production, with relatively low cost.

Ice Storage Cooling Systems

One of the problems for energy supply companies is that the highest demand for electricity often coincides with the highest cooling demand.

The utilities would prefer to "flatten the curve" (to even out or flatten the measure of average daily energy demand). The fewer the number of peaks (high points of energy demand), the less the utilities have to bolster their power supply with expensive, supplemental fuels.

One way to reduce this peaking problem is to supplement a building's cooling capacity with an ice storage system.

An ice storage system has three components: a tank with liquid storage balls, a heat exchanger, and a compressor for cooling. The essence of the ice storage system is that the chilling and freezing of the ice balls occurs at night (when the cost of energy is lower due to lower demand). During the day, the cool temperatures, stored in the ice, are transmitted into the building's cooling system.*

CONCLUSION

The knowledge of environmental systems has become essential to the architect's design palette. Buildings that take advantage of natural systems such as sun, wind, rain, ground water, topography, and climate are more elegant solutions. Architectural designs that incorporate natural systems, in conjunction with contemporary technologies, are in the tradition of architects providing spatial solutions with the most innovative contemporary thinking available.

Buildings with this approach operate more efficiently, integrate effectively into their local environment, and tend to produce spaces that are more pleasing to work and live. Knowledge of integrated or holistic design principals is not a limitation but another set of tools to produce humane, efficient, healthy, and aesthetically compelling architecture.

---

*   Source: Peter F. Smith, Sustainability at the Cutting Edge, Jordan Hill, Oxford: Architectural Press, an Imprint of Elsevier Science, 2003.

LESSON 3 QUIZ

1. Sustainable design is primarily concerned with which of the following issues?

   I.   Economics
   II. Aesthetics
   III. Environment
   IV. Mechanical systems

   A. III
   B. I, II, and III
   C. I and III
   D. All of the above

2. *The Natural Step* is an approach to the environment that follows which of the following principles?

   I.   The biosphere affecting humans is a relatively stable and resilient zone that includes five miles into the earth's crust and five miles into the troposphere.
   II. Improved technologies have dramatically increased the number and quantity of available natural resources.
   III. Toxic substances released into either the sea or atmosphere will only influence areas adjacent to the toxic source.
   IV. Using building materials that are recycled is an adequate sustainable design approach.

   A. I
   B. II
   C. II and IV
   D. None of the above

3. The planning phase of a sustainably designed architectural project should include which of the following elements?

   I.   Native landscaping that is aesthetically pleasing and functional
   II. Designing structures in the floodplain that can resist the forces of flood waters
   III. Consideration of sun orientation, topographic relief, and the scale of adjacent buildings
   IV. Locating projects within existing neighborhoods that are adjacent to public transportation

   A. I and II
   B. I and III
   C. I, III, and IV
   D. All of the above

4. The Ahwahnee principles include which of the following ideas?

   I.   Communities with only residential use should be relegated to areas outside the central business district.
   II. Preserved open spaces should be either wildlife habitats or recreational areas.
   III. Transportation planning should include roads, pedestrian paths, bike paths, and mass transit systems.
   IV. Job creation and economic diversity is a desired goal.

   A. I
   B. II, III, and IV
   C. III and IV
   D. None of the above

5. Life cycle costing is an economic evaluation of architectural elements that includes which of the following factors?

   I. First cost

   II. Maintenance and operational costs

   III. Repair costs

   IV. Replacement cost

   A. I

   B. II, III, and IV

   C. II and IV

   D. All of the above

6. LEED is concerned with which of the following? Check all that apply.

   A. Indoor air quality

   B. Storm water

   C. Construction costs

   D. Tax benefits

   E. Innovative energy systems

   F. Aesthetic design

7. Which of the following is a consultant who might be employed in a sustainable design project?

   I. Wetlands engineer

   II. Energy commissioner

   III. Landscape architect

   IV. Energy modeling engineer

   A. I

   B. I and II

   C. II, III, and IV

   D. All of the above

8. Sustainable design may require research and education that is beyond a normal architectural project. Which of the following is part of this process?

   I. Energy modeling

   II. Education of the client

   III. Art selection

   IV. Selection of energy efficient appliances

   A. I and IV

   B. I and II

   C. I, II, and IV

   D. All of the above

9. Sensitivity to the nuances of site conditions is key to sustainable design. Which of the following are site conditions the architect should examine in the design process?

   I. Solar orientation

   II. Decorative landscaping

   III. Scale and style of adjacent structures

   IV. Ground water conditions

   A. I and II

   B. I, III, and IV

   C. I and III

   D. All of the above

10. Sustainably designed architecture requires attention to which of the following building elements?

    I. Solar shading devices

    II. Urban heat island effect

    III. Increased parking

    IV. Fenestration and glazing

    A. I, II, and IV

    B. I and IV

    C. I and II

    D. All of the above

Part II

The Graphic Vignettes

THE NCARB SOFTWARE

Introduction
Vignette Screen Layout
The Computer Tools

INTRODUCTION

There is a wide variety of programs used by candidates at the firms in which they work. Therefore, an essential part of every candidate's preparation is to practice using the examination's computer tools. Candidates can download this software from the NCARB Web site (*www.ncarb.org*). This program contains tutorials and sample vignettes for all the graphic portions. Spend all the time necessary to become familiar with this material in order to develop the necessary technique and confidence. You must become thoroughly familiar with the software.

The drafting program for the graphic portions is by no means a sophisticated program. While this may frustrate candidates accustomed to advanced CAD software, it is important to recall that NCARB aimed to create an adequate drafting program that virtually anyone can use, even those with no CAD background at all.

VIGNETTE SCREEN LAYOUT

Each vignette has a number of sections and screens with which the candidate must become familiar. The first screen that appears when the vignette is opened is called the Vignette Index and starts with the Task Information Screen. Listed on this screen are all the components particular to this vignette. Each component opens a new screen when the candidate clicks on it with the mouse. A menu button appears in the upper left corner of any of these screens that returns you to the Index Screen. Also available from the Index Screen is a screen that opens the General Test Directions Screen, which gives the candidate an overview of the procedures for doing the vignettes. Here are the various screens found on the Index Screen:

■ **Vignette Directions** (found on all vignettes)—describes the procedure for solving the problem

■ **Program** (found on all vignettes)—describes the problem to be solved

■ **Tips** (found on all vignettes)—gives advice for approaching the problem and hints about the most useful drafting tools

■ **Code**—gives applicable code information if required by the vignette

■ **Sections**—typically found on the Stair Design Vignette and shows a section through the space in which the stair will be located

■ **Lighting Diagrams**—found on the Mechanical and Electrical Plan vignette to show light fixture distribution patterns

The beginning of each vignette lesson in this study guide provides a more detailed description of each vignette screen.

To access the actual vignette problem, press the space bar. This screen displays the problem and all the computer tools required to solve it. Toggle back and forth between the Vignette Screen and one of the screens from the Index Screen at any time by simply pressing the space bar. This is not as convenient as viewing both the drawing and, say, the printed program adjacent to each other at the same time. Thus it is a procedure that the candidate must become familiar with through practice. Also, some vignettes are too large to be displayed all at once on the screen. In this case use the scroll bars to move the screen up and down or left and right as needed. The Zoom Tool is also helpful.

THE COMPUTER TOOLS

There are two categories of computer tools found in the ARE graphic portions:

■ Common Tools
■ Tools specific to each vignette

The Common Tools, as the name implies, are generally present in all the tests and allow a candidate to draw lines, circles, and rectangles, adjust or move shapes, undo or erase a previously drawn object, and zoom to enlarge objects on the screen. There is also an on-screen calculator and a tool that lets you to erase an entire solution and begin again.

Vignette-specific tools include additional tools that enable the candidate to turn on and off layers, rotate objects, and set elevations or roof slopes. In addition to these extra tools, each vignette also includes specific items under the draw tool required for the vignette, such as joists or skylights. Become an expert in the use of each tool.

Each tool is dependent on the mouse, there are no "shortcut" keys on the keyboard. Press the computer tool first to activate it, then select the item or items on the drawing to be affected by the tool, and then re-click the computer tool to finish the operation. Spend as much time as required to become completely familiar with this drafting program. The Common Tools section of the practice vignettes available from NCARB is particularly useful for helping you become familiar with the computer tools. Three things to note: the left mouse button activates all tools; there is no zoom wheel on the mouse, nor an associated tool on the program; and the shift key activates the Ortho Tool.

The standard computer tools and their functions are shown in Figure 4.1.

BRINGS UP A MENU OF ITEMS, SUCH AS
ROOMS, COLUMNS, DOORS, ETC.; SOME
MENU ITEMS, SUCH AS *JOISTS,* MAY LEAD
TO SUBMENU ITEMS, SUCH AS *SPACING*

CHANGES THE SIZE OR SHAPE OF
A SINGLE OBJECT, OR RELOCATES
A PREVIOUSLY DRAWN OBJECT

MOVES A SELECTED ARRANGEMENT
OF OBJECTS AS A GROUP

ROTATES PREVIOUSLY DRAWN OBJECTS

BRINGS UP A SUBMENU, ALLOWS ACCESS TO
OTHER LAYERS OR OTHER FLOOR PLANS, ALLOWS
MULTIPLE LAYERS TO BE VIEWED AT THE SAME
TIME OR JUST ONE LAYER TO BE ISOLATED

VERIFIES SEVERAL CRITICAL CONDITIONS,
SUCH AS OVERLAPPING SPACES

BRINGS UP A MENU OF HELPFUL TOOLS,
SUCH AS A *BACKGROUND GRID, LINES,
CIRCLES, RECTANGLES,* AND A MEANS
TO DETERMINE MEASUREMENTS

LIMITS MOST TOOLS TO STRICTLY
VERTICAL AND HORIZONTAL DIRECTIONS

ALLOWS ENLARGEMENT OF A PORTION OF A
DRAWING TO PRODUCE DETAILED WORK; EMPLOYS
A PICK BOX TO ENLARGE ONLY WHAT IS SELECTED AND
THE OPTION TO RETURN TO THE ORIGINAL VIEW BY
CLICKING ON THE TOOL A SECOND TIME

CHANGES CURSOR TO FULL SCREEN SIZE,
WHICH HELPS ALIGN OBJECTS

DELETES THE LAST OPERATION COMPLETED

REMOVES PREVIOUSLY DRAWN OBJECTS

PROVIDES INFORMATION FOR SELECTED
OBJECTS, SUCH AS *SIZE, AREA, ANGLE, ETC.*

BRINGS UP A SCIENTIFIC CALCULATOR;
CLICK TO DISPLAY, CLICK AGAIN TO HIDE

RETURNS TO THE PROGRAM SCREEN–
SERVES THE SAME FUNCTION AS THE SPACE
BAR ON THE COMPUTER KEY BOARD

ERASES ALL DRAWING FROM THE SCREEN TO
BEGIN A NEW SOLUTION, IT IS SUGGESTED THAT
THIS TOOL ONLY BE USED AS A LAST RESORT

SELECTS ANOTHER VIGNETTE IN THE SAME
SECTION OR ALLOWS AN EXIT FROM THE EXAM

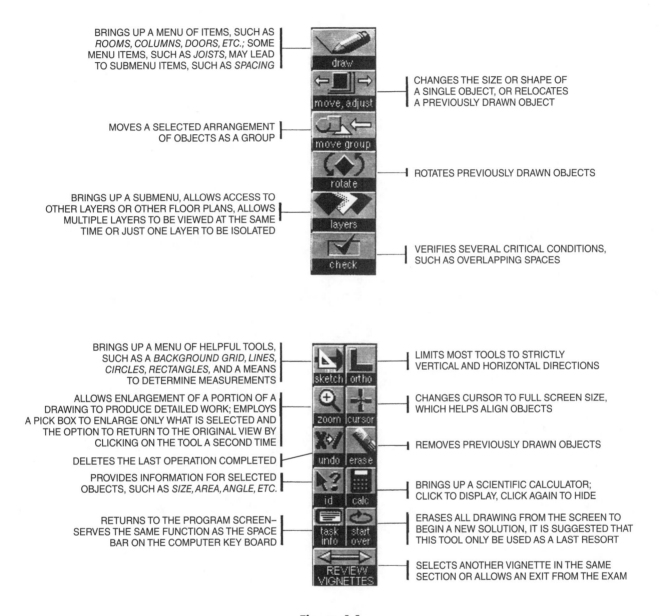

Figure 4.1

5

TAKING THE EXAM

INTRODUCTION

Preparation for the ARE usually begins several months before taking the actual exam. The first step is to submit an application for registration with your state board or Canadian provincial association. Most, but not all, registration boards require a professional degree in architecture and completion of the Intern-Development Program (IDP) before a candidate is allowed to begin the exam process. Since the processing of educational transcripts and employment verifications may take several weeks, begin this process early. The registration board will review a candidate's application to determine whether he or she meets the eligibility requirements.

SCHEDULING THE EXAM

The exams are available to eligible candidates at virtually any time, since test centers are open nearly every day throughout the year. However, it is the responsibility of the candidate to contact a test center to schedule an appointment. This must be done at least three days prior to the desired appointment time, but it is probably more sensible to make an appointment a month or more in advance. It is not necessary to take the test in the same jurisdiction in which you intend to be registered. Someone in San Francisco, for example, could conceivably combine his or her test-taking with a family visit in Philadelphia.

FINAL PREPARATION

Candidates are advised to complete all preparations the day before their appointment, in order to be as relaxed as possible before the upcoming test. Avoid last minute cramming, which in most cases does more harm than good. The exams not only test design competence, but also physical and emotional endurance. You must be totally prepared for the strenuous day ahead, and that requires plenty of rest and as much composure.

One of the principal ingredients for success on this exam is confidence. If you have prepared in a reasonable and realistic way, and if you have devoted the necessary time to practice, you should approach the Site Planning & Design division with confidence.

EXAM DAY

Woody Allen once said that a large part of being successful was just showing up. That is certainly true of the licensing examination, where you must not only show up, but also be on time. Get an early start on exam day and arrive at the test center at least 30 minutes before the scheduled test time. Getting an early start enables you to remain in control and maintain a sense of confidence, while arriving late creates unnecessary anxiety. If you arrive 30 minutes late, you may lose your appointment and forfeit the testing fee. Most candidates will begin their test session within one-half hour of the appointment time. You will be asked to provide a picture identification with signature and a second form of identification. For security reasons, you may also have your picture taken.

THE EXAM ROOM

Candidates are not permitted to bring anything (except a calculator) with them into the exam room: no reference materials, no scratch paper, no drawing equipment, no food or drink, no extra sweater, no cell phones, no digital watches. You are permitted to use the restroom or retrieve a sweater from a small locker provided outside the exam room. Each testing center will have its own procedure to follow for such needs. The candidate is allowed to bring his or her own non-programmable, non-printing, non-communicating scientific calculator. The test center staff reserve the right to not permit a calculator if they deem it necessary.

Some testing centers may have limited function handheld calculators available. In addition, a calculator is provided as part of the drafting program. Scratch paper will be provided by the testing center. The candidate might wish to request graph paper, if available.

Once the candidate is seated at an assigned workstation and the test begins, he or she must remain seated, except when authorized to leave by test center staff. When the first set of vignettes is completed, or time runs out, there is a mandatory break, during which you must leave the exam room. Photo identification will be required when you reenter the exam room for the next set of vignettes. At the conclusion of the test, staff members will collect all used scratch paper.

Exam room conditions vary considerably. Some rooms have comfortable seats, adequate lighting and ventilation, error-free computers, and a minimum of distractions. The conditions of other rooms, however, leave much to be desired. Unfortunately, there is little a candidate can do about this, unless, of course, his or her computer malfunctions. Staff members will try to rectify any problem within their control.

EXAM ROOM CONDUCT

NCARB has provided a lengthy list of offensive activities that may result in dismissal from a test center. Most candidates need not be concerned about these, but for those who may have entertained any of these fantasies, such conduct includes:

- Giving or receiving help on the test
- Using prohibited aids, such as reference material

- Failing to follow instructions of the test administrator
- Creating a disturbance
- Removing notes or scratch paper from the exam room
- Tampering with a computer
- Taking the test for someone else

BEGIN WITH THE PROGRAM

You can either solve the vignettes in the order they are presented or build confidence by starting with one that looks easier to you. Only you know what works best for you; the practice software should give you a sense of your preferred approach.

Every vignette solution begins with the program. Read the entire program carefully and completely, and consider every requirement. During this review, identify the requirements, restrictions, limitations, code demands, and other critical clues that will influence the solution. Feel free to use scratch paper to jot down key points, data, and requirements. This will help ensure that you understand and meet all the requirements as you develop your solution.

Every vignette problem has two components, the written program and a graphic base plan. Both components are complementary and equally important; together they completely define the problem. Candidates should not rush through a review of the program and base drawing in an attempt to begin the design sooner. It is more important to understand every constraint and to be certain that you have not overlooked any significant detail. Until you completely understand the vignette, it is pointless to continue.

GENERAL STRATEGIES

The approach to all vignette solutions is similar: Work quickly and efficiently to produce a solution that satisfies every programmatic requirement. The most important requirements are those that involve compliance with the code, such as life safety, egress, and barrier-free access.

Another important matter is design quality. Strive for an adequate solution that merely solves the problem. Exceptional solutions are not expected, nor are they necessary. You can only pass or fail this test, not win a gold medal. Produce a workable, error-free solution that is good enough to pass.

During the test session, candidates will frequently return to the program to verify element sizes, relationships, and specific restrictions. Always confirm program requirements before completing the vignette, so that oversights or omissions may be corrected while there is still time to do so. Candidates must always keep in mind the immutability of the program. That is, never—under any circumstances—modify, deviate from, or add anything to the program. Never try to *improve* the program. Lastly, taking time at the end of each section to review all the vignettes can help to eliminate small errors or omissions that could tip the balance between a passing and failing grade.

Candidates should have little trouble understanding a vignette's intent, however, the true meaning of certain details may be ambiguous and open to interpretation. Simply make a reasonable assumption and proceed with the solution.

While candidates will necessarily employ their own strategies for ordering the vignettes, what follows are some ideas others have found helpful.

1. Start with the vignette you feel most capable of completely quickly and competently. This will boost your confidence for the remaining vignettes.

2. Try to solve each problem in 10 minutes less than the allotted time. Use this additional time to review your solution.

3. Create a set of notes or a chart for each problem.

THE TIME SCHEDULE

The most critical problem on the exam is *time*, and you must use that fact as the organizing element around which any strategy is based. The use of a schedule is essential. During the preparation period, and especially after taking a mock exam, note the approximate amount of time that should be spent on each vignette solution. This information must then become a candidate's performance guide, and by following it faithfully, the candidate will automatically establish priorities regarding how his or her time will be spent.

It is important to complete each vignette in approximately the time allotted. You cannot afford to dwell on a minor detail of one vignette while completely ignoring another vignette. Forget the details, do not strive for perfection, and be absolutely certain to finish the test. Even the smallest attempt at solving a vignette will add points to your total score.

Vignettes have been designed so that a reasonable solution for each of the problems can be achieved in approximately the amount of time shown in the *ARE Guidelines*. These time limits are estimates made by those who created this test. In any event, a 45-minute-

long vignette may not necessarily take 45 minutes to complete. Some can be completed in 30 minutes, while others may take an hour or longer. The time required depends on the complexity of the problem and your familiarity with the subject matter. Some candidates are more familiar with certain problem types than others, and since candidates' training, experience, and ability vary considerably, adjustments may have to be made to suit individual needs. It should also be noted that within each exam section, the time allotted for two vignettes may be used at the candidate's discretion. For example, in a three-vignette section that allots 150 minutes, NCARB recommends spending one hour on one vignette and 45 minutes on the other two. However, you may actually spend 80 minutes on one problem and 35 minutes on the other two.

Candidates who are aware of the time limit are more able to concentrate on the tasks to be performed and the sequence in which they take place. You will also be able to recognize when to begin the next vignette. When the schedule tells you to stop working on one vignette and move on to the next, you will do so, regardless of the unresolved problems that may remain. You may submit an imperfect solution, but you *will* complete the test.

Only solve what the program asks you to solve, and don't use real world knowledge, such as specific building code requirements.

TIME SCHEDULE PROBLEMS

It is always possible that a candidate will be unable to complete a certain vignette in the time allotted. What to do in that event? First, avoid this kind of trouble by adhering to a rigid time schedule, regardless of problems that may arise. Submit a solution for every vignette, even if some solutions still have problems or are incomplete.

Candidates are generally able to develop some kind of workable solution in a relatively short time. If each decision is based on a valid assumption and relies on common sense, the major elements should be readily organized into an acceptable functional arrangement. It may not be perfect, and it will certainly not be refined, but it should be good enough to proceed to the next step.

MANAGING PROBLEMS

There are other serious problems that may arise, and while each is potentially fatal, they must be managed and resolved. Consider the following:

- The candidate has inadvertently omitted a major programmed element.

- The candidate has drawn a major element too large or too small.

- The candidate has ignored a critical adjacency or other relationship.

The corrective action for each of these issues will depend on the seriousness of the error and when the mistake is discovered. If there is time, one should rectify the design by returning to the point at which the error occurred and begin again from there. If it is late in the exam and time is running out, there may simply be insufficient time to correct the problem. In that case, continue on with the remainder of the exam and attempt to provide the most accurate solutions for the remaining vignettes. The best strategy, of course, is to avoid critical mistakes in the first place, and those who concentrate and work carefully will do so.

WORKING UNDER PRESSURE

The time limit of the exams creates subjective as well as real problems. This exam generates a unique psychological pressure that can be harmful to performance. While some designers thrive and do their best work under pressure, others become fearful or agitated under the same conditions. It is perfectly normal to be uneasy about this important event; and although anxiety may be a common reaction, it is still uncomfortable.

Candidates should be aware that pressure is not altogether a negative influence. It may actually heighten awareness and sharpen abilities. In addition, realize that, as important as this test may be, failure is not a career-ending event. Furthermore, failure is rarely an accurate measure of design ability; it simply means that you have not yet learned how to pass this difficult exam.

EXAMINATION ADVICE

Following is a short list of suggestions intended to help candidates develop their own strategies and priorities. We believe each item is important in achieving a passing score. The *ARE Guidelines,* available from the NCARB Web site, also lists suggestions for examination preparedness.

- **Get an early start.** Begin preparation early enough to develop confidence by the time you are scheduled to take the exam. Arrive at the exam site early and be ready to go when the test begins.

- **Complete all vignettes.** Incomplete solutions risk failure. Complete every problem, even if every detail is not complete or perfect.

- **Don't modify the program.** Never add, change, improve, or omit anything from a program statement. Never assume that there is an error in the program. Verify all requirements to ensure complete compliance with every element of the program. If ambiguities exist in the program, make a reasonable assumption and complete your solution.

- **Develop a reasonable solution.** Since most vignettes generally have one preferred solution, solve the problem in the most direct and reasonable way. Never search for a unique or unconventional solution, because on this exam, creativity is not rewarded.

- **Be aware of time.** The strict time constraint compels you to be a clock-watcher. Never lose sight of how much time you are spending on each vignette. When it is time to proceed to the next problem, quit and move on to the next vignette.

- **Remain calm.** This may be easier said than done, because this type of experience often creates stress in even the most self-assured candidate. Anxiety is generally related to fear of failure. However, if a candidate is well prepared, this fear may be unrealistic. Furthermore, even if the worst comes to pass and you must repeat a division, all it means is that your architectural license will be delayed for a short period of time.

SITE DESIGN VIGNETTE

INTRODUCTION

Site Design is a comprehensive exercise that tests your understanding of general site planning principles, including parking, building placement within building limits of the site, and site circulation. Candidates must develop a site plan based on a program that includes a number of specific building elements, site influences, parking and circulation requirements, and legal restrictions. You must integrate these program-matic demands, code restrictions, vehicular site access issues, parking requirements, and environmental considerations into a workable and logical design. Solutions will be analyzed for compliance with program requirements, completeness, and technical accuracy.

VIGNETTE INFORMATION

The Site Design vignette begins with an index screen, which offers the choice of several additional screens containing necessary information. Among these are:

- **General test directions**—This general information appears on the index screen of every Site Planning problem. Since it applies to all vignettes, candidates need not refer to it more than once. The screen includes the following advice:

   1. Read all directions and become familiar with the scope and nature of the problem.
   2. Ignore all other codes or standards that may be in conflict.
   3. Make no assumption of conditions unless they are specifically stated.
   4. Your initial solution may be developed on screen with computer tools or on scratch paper.

5. No reference material is permitted other than what is on the screen.

6. No paper may be used other than that provided.

- **Vignette Directions**—These offer instructions about preparing your site design. It describes the site on which to place the buildings, parking lot, related site elements, and vegetation. One is advised that the location of all elements must relate to the existing environmental conditions. The programmed elements are listed as follows:

  1. Buildings

  2. Outdoor space

  3. Parking spaces

  4. Pedestrian walkways

  5. Vehicular access and service drive

  6. Vegetation

- **Program**—This screen contains a description of each required element, including specific adjacencies, orientation, and restrictions. The height of the buildings and size of the open space are specified, as is the number of required car spaces. Other data include orientation regarding sun, wind, and views, vehicular and pedestrian circulation requirements, and any other detail affecting the layout, such as the number of permitted curb cuts.

- **Tree Diagrams**—Illustrated here are the diameter and height (in plan and elevation) of both deciduous and coniferous trees that may appear on the given site.

- **Tips**—These are suggestions, generally regarding specific computer tools that help the candidate work more effectively. For instance, use the *move group* tool to move a bank of parking spaces, and make minor adjustments to elements with the *zoom*

tool. The tips area might also suggest that parking spaces be laid out to the proper scale, the dimensions of which may be read directly in the *element information* area of the screen. You can then rotate or reposition spaces with the *rotate* tool or *move group* tool. Other useful tools for the Site Design vignette that this screen might highlight include the *move, adjust* tool to modify the position or size of drives or sidewalks, and the *sketch line* tool to layout clearances. A final helpful tip that the this screen will most likely emphasize is that road and drives are joined by connecting their dashed centerlines.

The work screen, on which your solution is actually presented, is displayed by pressing the space bar on the computer keyboard. One may toggle between this screen and any other screen in the same way. The work screen contains the site plan that shows existing roads, property lines, building limit lines, easements, trees and other natural features, wind direction, and north arrow. Site contours are not indicated, since topography is not a part of the Site Design problem. Along the left side of this screen are found the computer tool icons, including the draw tool, which brings up the list of required elements.

DESIGN PROCEDURE

The Site Design vignette requires candidates to arrange in plan a number of elements that conform to the programmatic requirements. The resulting solution will be a schematic plan, not unlike those produced each day in most architectural offices. Diagrams such as these are simple in appearance, and most can be developed in a relatively short time. Buildings are represented by simple rectangles, and paved open spaces, roads, and parking areas are shown as simple geometric shapes defined by single solid lines.

Some specific hints regarding the parking area portion of this vignette will be helpful. Before laying out the actual parking spaces, have an idea of where on the site the parking lot will be located. In this regard, a quick pencil sketch may be helpful. This initial placement is dictated by (1) the location of the buildings and open space to be served, (2) the position of the access street, and (3) the relationship the parking lot will have with other site elements, such as trees or a pond.

Once you have determined the location of the parking lot, the buildings, and the open space, lay out the parking lot as a double-loaded corridor arrangement. This will use the least amount of the site area and minimize pavement. Parking layouts often employ drive-through circulation. This means that a driver will enter the site at a specific location along the access street, drive through the parking area, and exit the site along the same or possibly a second driveway to the street. During this process the driver will continue to move in only one direction; there will be no dead-ends and it should never be necessary to drive in reverse.

Parking spaces are drawn using the *Parking Spaces* or *Accessible Space* draw tool. When candidates click on either of these tools, they will see a box that allows them to select the number of continuous spaces desired. Select ten, for example, and you will be able to lay out ten spaces, with the dimensions appearing in the *element information area* as you move the cursor. So, if the required car slot is 9 feet by 18 feet, using this tool to layout a rectangle that is 90 feet in one direction (10 × 9) and 18 feet in the other. At that point, the individual car spaces will automatically appear in the rectangle. Roads are laid out as double lines with

the proper width previously programmed. The *draw* tool will allow you to layout the road, with turns or bends in any direction.

Save the placement of trees until all other site elements have been located. Be careful to pay attention to the allowable number of existing trees the program indicates can be removed.

ANALYZING THE SITE PLAN

The solution to a Site Design vignette begins with an analysis of the site plan. A candidate must identify and analyze those conditions that will affect the arrangement of elements on the site. For example:

- If a building entrance is required to receive the noonday summer sun, position that entrance to face due south.
- A service entrance, blocked from pedestrian view, might be necessary for one of the buildings. Position it away from public areas, or place a row of coniferous trees to screen the service drive.
- One of buildings might require a view of a pond. Again, this will affect the arrangement of the elements on the site.

Each site requirement or limitation that can be identified will further define your solution and help determine where key plan elements are placed. Some restrictions will be obvious; a utility easement, for example, will indicate that no construction may occur over the easement area. Similarly, the building limit lines will act as boundaries to your design, beyond which no development may occur. Driveways and pedestrian walks may cross setbacks, of course, but no other development is permitted in setback areas.

Some sites may contain a number of randomly spaced trees. These are placed on the site to create obstacles around which your design must be fitted. In many cases, one is permitted to remove a certain number of existing trees to make the site layout less troublesome. One should not hesitate to remove all the trees allowed, because your solution will come more easily and, in addition, no extra credit is given for removing fewer than the number of trees permitted.

IMPORTANT PARKING OBJECTIVES

There are several ways to run into serious problems in laying out the parking lot in the Site Design vignette. In the interest of avoiding these pitfalls, we offer the following suggestions:

- Never create a dead-end parking arrangement; that is, one in which a driver must back up to reach another part of the parking area or the exit.

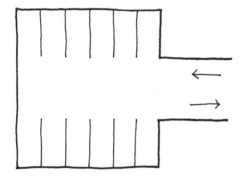

DEAD-END PARKING

Figure 6.1

- Be certain that the flow of traffic through the parking area is continuous in one direction.

- Always locate the required handicapped parking spaces as close as possible to the entrance of the existing building. It should be obvious that the disabled should walk the shortest distance from their cars to the building.

- Always locate the required handicapped parking spaces so that the disabled are not forced to cross roads or traffic aisles or circulate behind parked cars.

- Always use parking spaces that are perpendicular to (never parallel with) the traffic aisle.

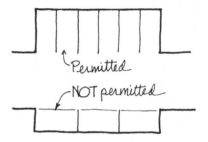

PERPENDICULAR AND PARALLEL PARKING

Figure 6.2

- Be certain that your access driveway is perpendicular to the existing street for at least the distance specified in the program. The reason for this is safety; a driver should be able to turn with equal ease from either direction when entering or exiting the site. It is not uncommon for an access street to run at an angle to the other sides of the site. Therefore, the rectangular parking area may be parallel to three sides of the site, but the driveway from the street will always be perpendicular to the street for some distance.

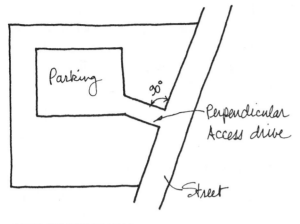

ACCESS DRIVEWAY

Figure 6.3

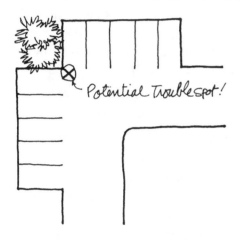

DANGEROUS CORNER PARKING

Figure 6.4

■ A compact and efficient parking layout is highly desirable. However, at right-angled corners, one should never place parking spaces so close to one another that either car could cause an accident when leaving the space.

■ If a passenger drop-off area is required, be certain the passenger side of the car ends up adjacent to the drop-off area.

■ When avoiding existing trees, be certain that no paved surface encroaches within the drip line of any tree.

ARRANGING THE ELEMENTS

The elements comprising this vignette are listed under the *draw* tool, and clicking on any listed term will allow you to draw that required element. For example, if you click on the term *Classroom Building*, you will be able to drag the prescribed building shape, complete with title, height of structure, and entrance indicated, to any location on the site. You will have no control over the shape of this element; it is predetermined and all you can do is locate it on the site. If, after locating this element, you want to change its position, you may do so with the *move*, *adjust* tool or with the *rotate* tool. In other words, every required structure may be quickly placed on the site and then arranged later in a final composition.

The elements of this vignette are listed under the *draw* tool in a specific order, and it is probably best to consider each element in that same order. That means the structures will be located first, then the paved plaza or open space, then parking spaces, followed by the driveway(s) and pedestrian walkways, and finally the trees. The position of any element may be adjusted or rotated at any time, so the initial placement is not critical. Nevertheless, a candidate will save a great deal of time if he or she has some notion of how the elements relate to one another, as well as an understanding of all the programmatic restrictions.

CIRCULATION

An essential element of the Site Design vignette is circulation; pedestrians and vehicles must be able to get where they are going safely and efficiently. Most problems require a continuous pedestrian walkway system that includes a paved plaza area off which are the building entrances. The vehicular circulation system begins with access from an adjacent street. The driveway should be perpendicular to the street, and it should lead directly to (1) any or all of the building entrances, (2) the parking area, and (3) the required service entrance. The service drive must generally be kept separate from the parking area. Parking areas should be designed for one-way traffic, as far as possible, and pedestrians should be able to circulate safely from the parking area to the buildings.

FINAL ARRANGEMENT

When you are reasonably satisfied with your schematic arrangement, go back to the program and verify every restriction.

Some items to check:

- Do the buildings have the required adjacencies and view?
- Are all the components on the site the required distance apart from each other?
- Does the open plaza allow pedestrians access to each of the structures?
- Have the building entrances been shielded from the prevailing winds?
- Has the service entrance—if called for—been blocked from view?
- Have the required number of accessible spaces been met?
- Have all parking lot pitfalls been avoided?
- Have more trees been removed than allowed?
- Do any of the site elements encroach beyond the setbacks?
- Are the easements respected?

Candidates must answer all these questions and verify that there are no encroachments beyond setback lines or easements. To achieve a passing grade, follow every requirement of the program and solve the problem directly and simply.

KEY COMPUTER TOOLS

- **Draw Tool** All the key components of the site plan are included in the draw tool's sub-menu.
- **Move/Adjust** The candidate will find it absolutely necessary to use this tool for moving components around on the site while trying to arrive at their most advantageous location.
- **Move Group** At times it might be helpful to move multiple elements at the same time.
- **Rotate** An essential tool for positioning the requisite items on the site.
- **Sketch Tool** Use this tool to lay out parking spaces and distances from adjacent elements on site.
- **Zoom Tool** The Zoom tool will be especially helpful for locating the parking lot and driveway accurately on site.

VIGNETTE 1 SITE DESIGN

Introduction

The following Site Design practice vignette includes both general site planning components found on previous Site Design vignettes and a parking lot exercise that is very similar to the stand-alone Site Parking vignettes that were part of previous versions of the ARE. Included in this lesson's narrative is a thorough discussion of all the components of site design: building location, pedestrian open space, parking lot, and vegetation requirements. This study exercise is similar in scope, specifics, and the degree of difficulty that the candidate will encounter on the actual computer examination. The candidate is encouraged to read through this introductory material, do the practice problem, then read the detailed discussion that follows describing the design process and suggested solutions. This will help you gain a better understanding of the recommended approach and design sequencing.

Candidates often wonder where and how to begin a vignette solution. With so little time available, we believe that knowing where to start and what procedures to follow is essential to passing this examination. Without a plan or method, there is little hope of success. Those who are prepared will solve the problem in a direct and logical way, while those using a hit-or-miss approach will waste a good deal of time trying to decide what to do next.

We urge candidates to study the following design procedures. Our solution is certainly not the only possible one, but it evolved through a logical process. If you understand this process, you should be able to apply these concepts to any similar problem.

The Exam Sheet

The site plan is the same one on which a candidate was required to present his or her solution. Our problems were originally presented on 12″ × 18″ tracing paper sheets, and most were drawn at a scale of 1″ = 40′. The vignettes in this lesson, however, have been reduced to fit the course format, and therefore their scale is 1″ = 50′. On the actual exam, scale is relative and generally unimportant. In fact, the appearance of elements may vary with the size of the computer screen.

The program presents relatively simple requirements for a new Church Complex. There are three principal components organized around a Courtyard, but since the Church and Fellowship Hall are combined in a single structure, there are really only two individual buildings to consider. Besides the buildings and Courtyard, the program includes a Parking Area and circulation elements, such as a driveway and pedestrian walks.

VIGNETTE 1 SITE DESIGN

You are to develop a schematic site plan for a new church based on the requirements that follow. The program includes three principal components organized around a central courtyard: worship space, education space, and fellowship space. The required components shall be used as drawn, but they may be rotated.

1. In addition to the required components, provide a Courtyard that is 10,000 square feet in size and which provides direct access to the two structures. Locate the Fountain in the Courtyard.

   ■ The Courtyard shall be protected from prevailing winds by means of buildings and/or trees.

   ■ Provide a 40-foot-long minimum passenger drop-off at the Courtyard.

   ■ Provide pedestrian access to the Courtyard from the street.

2. Locate the School no closer to the Church than 25 feet.

   ■ The School shall have a view of the existing stream.

3. All driveways shall be 25 feet wide, and circulation shall be essentially one-way.

   ■ A maximum of two curb cuts are permitted.

   ■ Indicate the pattern of all vehicular circulation.

   ■ The service drive may be 15 feet wide, and no turnaround is necessary.

   ■ The service access shall be hidden from view, as far as possible.

4. Provide parking for 25 cars parked at 90 degrees, as follows:

   ■ 22 10-foot × 20-foot standard spaces.

   ■ 3 15-foot × 20-foot universally accessible spaces.

   ■ All parking shall be within building limit lines, and dead-end parking shall not be allowed.

   ■ The parking area shall be screened from both the Courtyard and Deacon Drive.

5. Additional requirements:

   ■ The church entrance should be visible from Deacon Drive.

   ■ No improvements may occur within setbacks or in conflict with existing site features, except driveways and walks may cross setbacks to connect to public access.

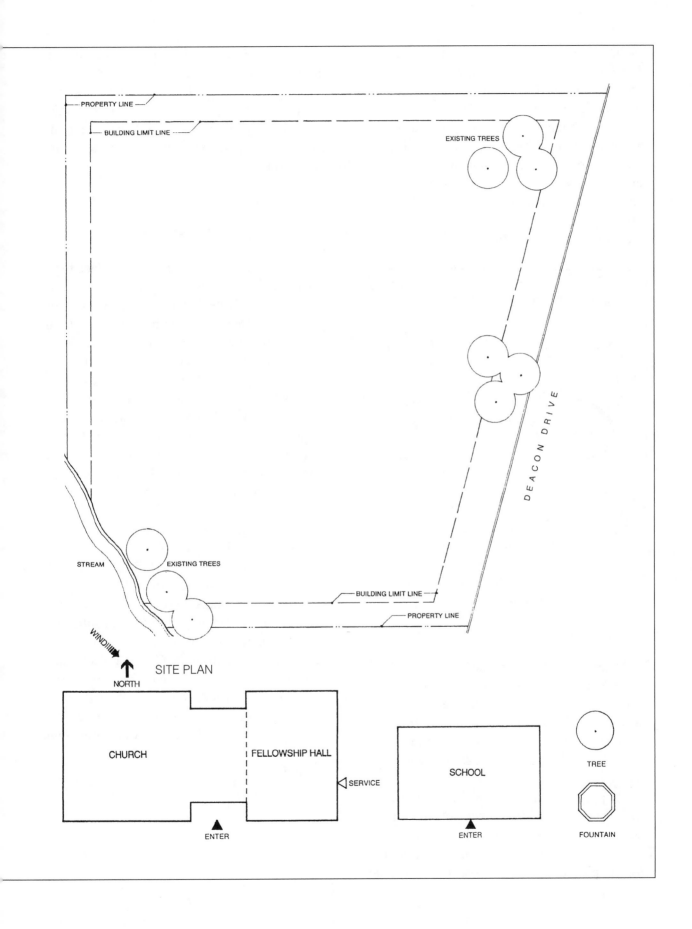

PROPERTY LINE

BUILDING LIMIT LINE

EXISTING TREES

DEACON DRIVE

STREAM

EXISTING TREES

BUILDING LIMIT LINE

PROPERTY LINE

WIND

NORTH

SITE PLAN

CHURCH

FELLOWSHIP HALL

SERVICE

ENTER

SCHOOL

ENTER

TREE

FOUNTAIN

Graphic representations of the required components of this problem are shown. The two structures must be used as drawn; however, they may be rotated into another position. Also shown are a Fountain, which will be placed somewhere in the Courtyard, and a typical tree to be used to block the wind or an unsightly view. The only important element not shown is the Courtyard, whose area is specified as 10,000 square feet, which is about the size of the Church/Fellowship Hall structure.

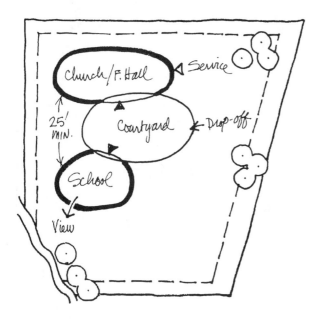

BUBBLE DIAGRAM OF BUILDING LAYOUT

Figure 6.5

Site Analysis

Candidates should analyze the site to identify those elements that affect the placement of elements on the site. We first notice that there is a single access street, Deacon Drive, from which all pedestrian and vehicular traffic will come. This will have a significant impact on the location of the access drive and parking lot. The program states that the School must have a view of a stream, and we note that this stream is at the southwest corner of the site. There are a few existing trees on the site, and these are placed here as hazards, similar to sand

traps on a golf course. One must work around them, since they must not be encroached upon or removed. Building limit lines are shown, and all development must be contained within these. Finally, we note the north arrow pointing straight up and the wind direction pointing to the southeast.

Bubble Diagram

It is generally best to locate the largest structure first, in this case, the Church/Fellowship Hall. The only restrictions are that it must face the Courtyard and that its entrance must be visible from Deacon Drive. We assume the Courtyard will be near Deacon Drive, because pedestrian access is required to the Courtyard from the street. Therefore, we begin by locating the Church/Fellowship Hall at the northwest corner of the site. We are not yet certain of the building's orientation. The entrance may face south or east, which means that the service entrance will face east or north. At this location, we have sufficient room to place the School toward the southwest corner, where it can overlook the stream.

We next locate the School south of the Church/Fellowship Hall, where it will be close enough to the stream to have the required view. However, it must be at least 25 feet from the Church/Fellowship Hall. The School entrance must face north or east, so that it can be accessed directly from the Courtyard. We can now lay out the 10,000-square-foot Courtyard, which incorporates the entrances of both buildings. Regarding this element, or any paved open space you are given, always assume it will be a rectangle whose proportions are between 1:1 and 2:1.

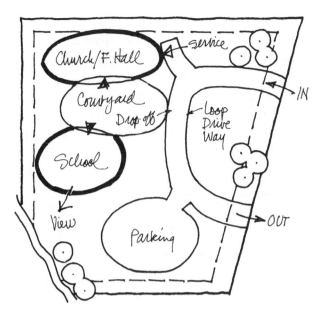

BUBBLE DIAGRAM WITH CIRCULATION

Figure 6.6

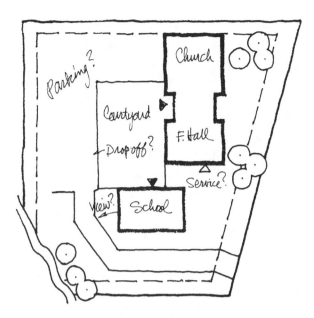

UNWORKABLE SOLUTION

Figure 6.7

Circulation

Our next concern is the vehicular circulation on the site. The program calls for one-way traffic, and two curb cuts are permitted. From these two facts, one should immediately visualize cars entering the site at either the north or south end of Deacon Drive and exiting at the opposite end. How do we decide which end will be the entrance and which the exit? The answer lies with the requirement for a 40-foot-long passenger drop-off at the Courtyard. To position the passenger side of the car along the Courtyard, cars must enter the site at the north and exit at the south. Thus, we create a driveway loop off of Deacon Drive that is adjacent to the Courtyard. These are the only two curb cuts permitted; therefore, the Parking Area and service drive must somehow connect to this driveway loop. Since the Service Drive must attach to the Fellowship Hall, we assume that the Service Drive will head northward, while the Parking Area will be located at the southern end of the site.

Diagrammatic Arrangements

Much of the site analysis discussed above may be no more than a mental process, and candidates may not have the time or the need to draw the assumed location of every element. It will generally be sufficient to use common sense in eliminating most possibilities. For example, if one considered locating the structures along Deacon Drive, it would be immediately apparent that the Courtyard would have to be west of the buildings, and thus, the building entrances would be out of sight from the street. In addition, the Courtyard would be completely unprotected from the prevailing winds, and the vehicular circulation and parking would be difficult to arrange. You do not have to draw solutions such as these, because it should be obvious that they do not work.

With the position of the major elements determined, we can now proceed to design the site. As shown in the first diagrammatic sketch (Figure 6.8), we locate the Church/Fellowship Hall at the northwest corner of the site, and the

School is placed 25 feet south of that structure, close to the stream. The building entrances are 90 degrees to one another and connected by the rectangular Courtyard. The position of the two structures will protect the Courtyard from the prevailing winds. We then locate the access driveway adjacent to the Courtyard to provide for the passenger drop-off. The northern end of the driveway turns into a Service Drive which runs to the Fellowship Hall. The Parking Area in this scheme is placed along Deacon Drive, across the driveway from the Courtyard.

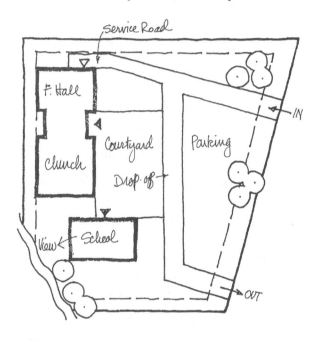

1ST DIAGRAMMATIC SCHEME

Figure 6.8

This diagrammatic scheme in Figure 6.8 solves most of the problems, but a remaining problem is the location of the Parking. First, the view of cars is all one sees from Deacon Drive. More serious, however, is that all drivers must cross the driveway to reach the buildings. This kind of circulation is unsafe and undesirable.

The diagrammatic sketch in Figure 6.9 shows the Church/Fellowship Hall at the same northwest corner, but rotated 90 degrees. The Courtyard separates the two structures, and the

School's view of the stream is maintained. The loop driveway provides access to the Service Road, Courtyard drop-off, and Parking Area, which has moved to the southern part of the site. In all, this arrangement works fairly well; however, the Courtyard is exposed to the prevailing winds and the Parking Area is just a bit too small.

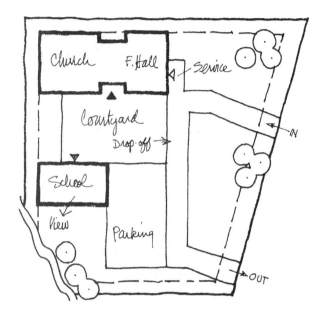

2ND DIAGRAMMATIC SCHEME

Figure 6.9

Our final diagrammatic sketch (Figure 6.10) is a refinement of the previous arrangement. The Church/Fellowship Hall has moved to the east; the School is located 25 feet to the south and rotated 90 degrees. The Courtyard accommodates the entrances of the two buildings, and the Parking Area is now larger and located directly south of the Courtyard. The looped driveway remains, and we have added the required pedestrian walk. Vehicles now enter the site at about the middle of Deacon Drive, turn right for the service drive or left for the 40-foot-long passenger drop-off, and then continue south to the Parking Area. This layout also allows vehicles to exit the property at the south end of Deacon Drive without having to drive through the parked cars.

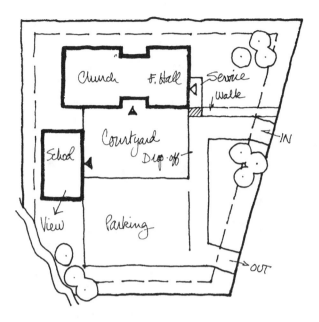

3RD DIAGRAMMATIC SCHEME
Figure 6.10

Potential Problems

At this point, we should review the program to be certain all the elements are there, and that we have not created any insurmountable problems. We note that the service drive, which is required to be hidden from view, faces directly onto Deacon Drive. This will probably have to be screened by trees, because to rotate the building and face the service access northward would cause even more serious problems.

Another potential problem is locating the pedestrian access from the street to the Courtyard. Regardless of where we place the walk, pedestrians must cross the driveway to reach the Courtyard. This could create a hazardous situation, and therefore, the problem must be solved when we make our final layout.

Final Site Design

Our final Site Design is shown superimposed over the site plan on the first preprinted sheet. (See Figure 6.11.) The elements are shown to

scale, and all the other requirements have been completed. For example, the Parking Area is shown with the required 25 cars, including the three handicapped spaces located as close as possible to the Courtyard. The Parking Area was to be shielded from both the Courtyard and Deacon Drive, and this is accomplished by adding two screens of trees.

Vehicular circulation is shown as previously planned, and traffic is indicated by means of directional arrows. It is essentially one-way traffic that begins at Deacon Drive, passes by the passenger drop-off, and then continues to the Parking Area or to the exit at the southern end of Deacon Drive. The new pedestrian walk from the street was placed just north of the entrance driveway. Where it crosses the narrow service road, we have indicated hatching, which recognizes our concern for this less than perfect situation. Our reasoning here is that the service drive traffic will be less frequent and busy than that of the main driveway. It is always best to keep pedestrians and vehicles widely separated, but with this arrangement, that was not possible.

Finally, we placed the required Fountain near the center of the Courtyard, on the axis of the Church/Fellowship Hall entrance. The shape of the Fountain indicates that this is an element without a front or back and probably equally interesting from all sides. Thus, it should be placed where pedestrians can circulate around it.

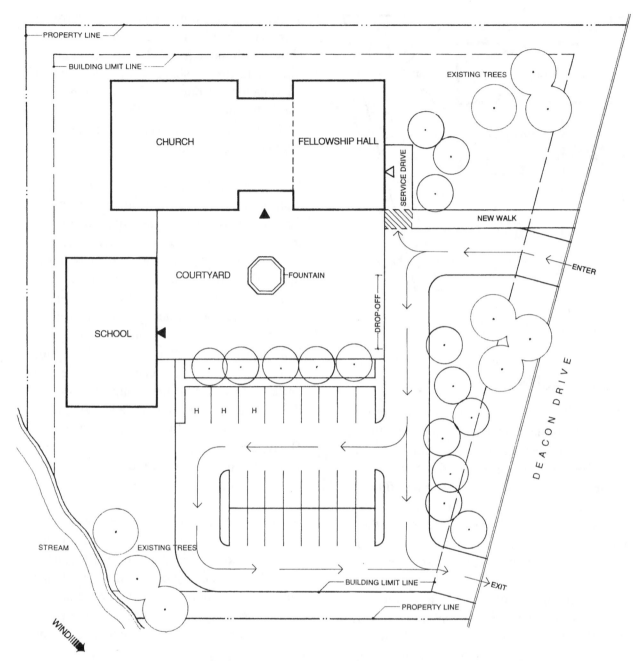

SITE DESIGN VIGNETTE - SUGGESTED SOLUTION

Figure 6.11

SITE GRADING VIGNETTE

INTRODUCTION

You are given a program and a site plan that includes existing contours, landscaping features, and manmade elements. You are then asked to modify the existing contours to accommodate the given elements and satisfy the drainage requirements and other restrictions of the program. Solutions are analyzed for compliance with the programmatic requirements, completeness, and technical accuracy.

VIGNETTE INFORMATION

The Site Grading vignette begins with an index screen from which one may access the other information screens as follows:

- **Vignette Directions**—The directions on this screen are brief and quite simple. You are told that the accompanying topographic representation of an existing site is to be regraded. You are then directed to modify the contours so that water will flow from the site according to the program and site conditions.

- **Program**—This screen describes the manmade elements around which water must be made to flow. These generally include paved elements, structures, and landscaping features, all of which must remain undisturbed by the contour modification. You are also told that the regraded site is limited to a specific maximum slope.

- **Tips**—This screen tells a candidate very little. It notes that the *erase* tool affects all changes made to a contour, while the *undo* tool affects only the last action. The most important tip that is inexplicably missing concerns the *move, adjust* tool, which is the one tool that is vitally needed to revise existing contours.

The preprinted site plan, on which you must present your solution, is found on the work screen, which you can access by touching the space bar on the computer keyboard. The site indicates the bordering property lines, complete contours, landscape features, and man-made elements. Nothing more is shown, nor is anything more necessary to solve this problem. The abbreviated tool icons are shown along the left side of the screen, since there is essentially only one tool that will be used to solve the problem.

DESIGN PROCEDURE

The Site Grading vignette requires a candidate to modify the contours on a site in order to drain the surface water in a specific manner. Generally, there will be a paved area and some trees that must remain undisturbed, while the contours are manipulated so that the surface water is directed around them. Therefore, while the title of this vignette is Site Grading, it might just as well have been Site Drainage.

You cannot even begin a solution to this problem without knowing the principles of contour manipulation for the purposes of grading and drainage. Some of the important principles are listed below:

1. To begin with, a *contour* is an imaginary line that connects points of equal elevation. If, for example, a contour were labeled 125, every point along that contour line would be at the identical elevation 125.

2. *Existing contours* are generally shown with a dashed line, while modified or *finish contours* are shown with a solid line.

3. The *contour interval* is the uniform difference in elevation between adjacent contours. In most vignette problems, the contour interval will be one or two feet.

4. Contours that are close together represent a *steep slope*, whereas contours further apart represent a *shallow slope*.

5. Contours that are evenly spaced represent a *uniform slope*. This is an important configuration when creating a consistently sloped driveway, parking area, or pedestrian walk.

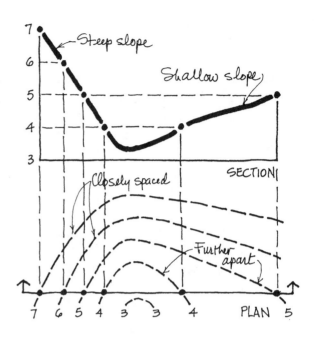

VALLEY CONFIGURATION

Figure 7.1

6. Contours that point uphill represent a *valley*. This is an essential configuration when solving drainage problems, because one creates valleys, or *swales*, to drain surface water. A common error on this vignette is for a candidate to mistakenly point the contours downhill. This creates ridges instead of swales, sheds water instead of channeling it, and always leads to a failing grade.

7. Surface water always flows in a direction perpendicular to contours.

A *swale* is a small valley-like configuration used to drain surface water in a specific direction. Try to maintain uniformly spaced contours in a swale to assure that the drained water flows at a consistent speed. Swales are generally depicted as steep, open triangles with a narrow rounded end pointing uphill. Using the ARE computer program, however, the uphill end of each loop will always come to a point.

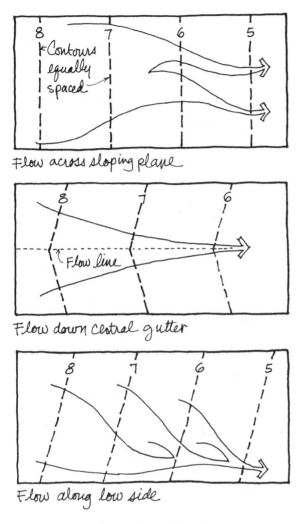

Flow across sloping plane

Flow down central gutter

Flow along low side

DRAINAGE OF PAVED SURFACES

Figure 7.2

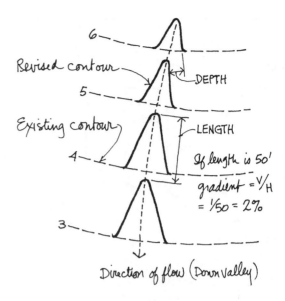

Revised contour — DEPTH

Existing contour — LENGTH

If length is 50'

gradient = V/H

= $1/50$ = 2%

Direction of flow (Down valley)

DRAINAGE SWALE

Figure 7.3

To drain surface water around a level area, a contour of a lower elevation must essentially surround the entire level area. For example, if the elevation of a terrace were 15, then the 14 contour would be drawn behind the terrace, and swales would be created to drain the surface water around the entire terrace. The lower elevation contour behind the terrace actually functions as a drainage ditch.

Since this is essentially a problem of creating drainage swales, you should become proficient in using the *move, adjust* tool. Proceed in the following way:

■ On the Site Grading site plan screen, click on the *move, adjust* tool. This will bring up a series of small squares that are centered along the length of every contour line. These squares are randomly spaced with apparently no relationship to one another.

■ Using the mouse, place the cross-shaped cursor over any of these squares and click once.

■ Clicking activates the square, which may then be dragged to a new position on the site. The part of the contour that is repositioned is that portion that lies between the two adjacent squares on the contour line.

■ Click again and the modified contour remains set in its new position on the site.

■ You may also reposition any square along the contour line itself. This is done in the same way as just described. The purpose of moving a square along its length is to control the shape of a contour in a swale, to make its wide end narrower or more open.

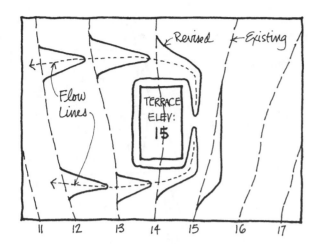

DRAINING SURFACE WATER
AROUND A LEVEL AREA

Figure 7.4

With some practice, candidates should be able to modify contours quickly and accurately. Not every contour, of course, will require modification. You should change only those that affect the drainage of surface water around the fixed landscape or manmade elements. Once the surface water has passed the element, the swale can end and the water will continue to drain downhill in an unguided fashion.

An important part of constructing drainage swales is controlling the slope of the regraded portions of the site. First, be aware of the maximum allowable slope. For example, the program might state that *regraded slopes may not exceed 20 percent*. In that event, modified contours with a contour interval of one foot would be spaced a *minimum* of five feet apart. The formula one uses is as follows: The Gradient = Vertical Component ÷ Horizontal Component, or in this case $1' \div 5' = 0.2$ or 20%.

Having determined the minimum allowable spacing between contours, such as five feet in the example above, you must then be certain that your regraded contours do not exceed that dimension. This may be verified with the use of several *sketch* tools. Using the *measure* and *line*

tools, distances may be determined directly and observed in the element information area at the bottom of the screen.

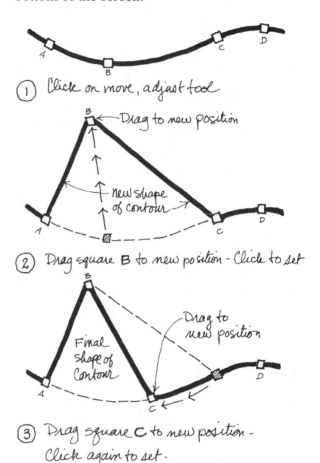

MODIFYING A COMPUTERIZED CONTOUR

Figure 7.5

Another and perhaps quicker way to verify contour spacing is as follows: Use the circle tool to construct a circle with a radius of 2.5 feet (a diameter of 5 feet), which is an amount that can be read in the element information area. That circle may then be used repeatedly to check the distance between contours at any number of points along a contour.

Some candidates may find it helpful to construct a swale flow line before actually constructing the swale. Use the *sketch line* tool to draw the pattern of flow around the vignette elements and down the site. This flow line then becomes the central spine on which the modified contour loops are arranged.

KEY COMPUTER TOOLS

■ **Move Tool** Critical to this vignette is the move tool. The candidate is advised to become very familiar with this tool in the practice exams as it can be a tricky tool to use.

VIGNETTE 2 SITE GRADING

A proposed parking plan has been superimposed over an existing site. You are to regrade the site and modify existing contours so that all surface water will flow to the storm drain inlet shown.

1. Draw revised contours over the paved parking lot so that surface water will be directed towards the storm drain inlet.

   ■ The 61 finish contour has been established at the paved driveway.

   ■ A 57 finish spot grade has been established at the north end of the paved parking area.

2. Draw revised contours on all sides of the paved parking area so that surface water from unpaved areas will not run over the paved parking area.

   ■ Direct all surface water toward the storm drain inlet.

3. Additional requirements:

   ■ Finish contours shall be continuous from one end of a property line to another.

   ■ The regraded slope on the paved parking lot shall not exceed 5 percent.

   ■ The regraded slope outside the parking lot shall not exceed 20 percent.

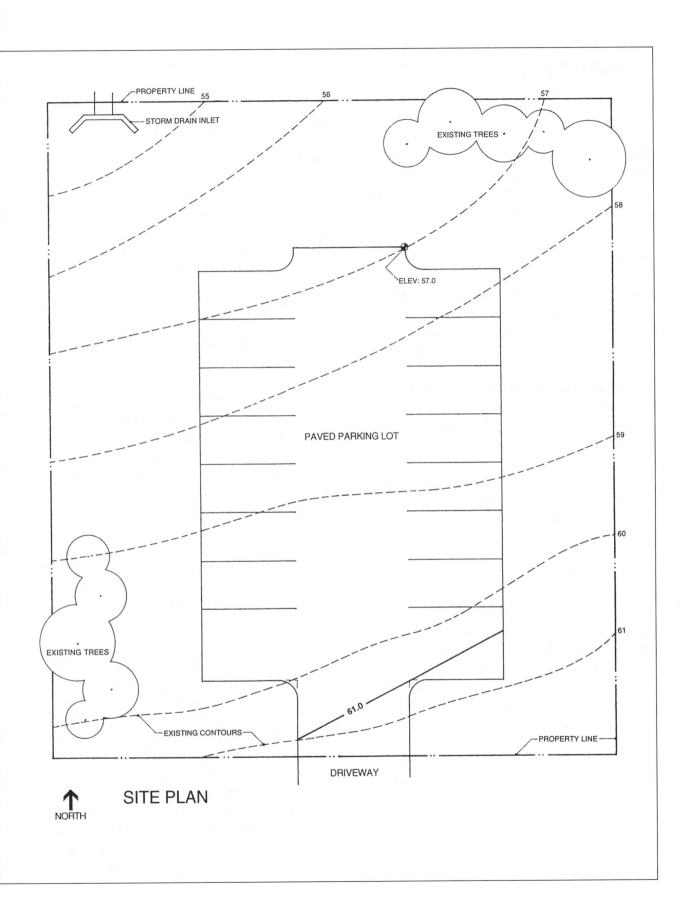

PROPERTY LINE
55
56
57
STORM DRAIN INLET
EXISTING TREES
58
ELEV: 57.0
PAVED PARKING LOT
59
60
61
EXISTING TREES
61.0
EXISTING CONTOURS
PROPERTY LINE
DRIVEWAY

↑
NORTH

SITE PLAN

VIGNETTE 2 SITE GRADING

Introduction

This vignette has many of the same elements and details found on the actual exam. What is more important, it will help you understand the connection between contour modification and the drainage of surface water from a site.

The Exam Sheet

Shown on the preceding pages are the program and site plan. The program describes a parking arrangement that has been superimposed over an existing site. You are asked to regrade the site and modify the existing contours so that surface water will flow to the storm drain inlet. Specifically, you are instructed to revise the contours over the paved area so that water is directed toward the drain.

You are further instructed to revise the contours around the paved parking area so that surface water from the unpaved areas will not run over the paving. Finally, we are told that regraded slopes may not exceed 5 percent at paved areas and 20 percent at other portions of the site.

The site plan shows a paved parking area for 16 cars superimposed over an existing rectangular site. The grade drops over six feet in elevation, from a little over 61 where the driveway meets the south property line, to the storm drain inlet at the northwest corner of the site. There are two existing tree clumps, at the northeast and southwest, and it must be assumed that these will remain undisturbed. The existing contours have a one-foot interval, and to get you started, you are given the revised contour 61 near the driveway and a spot elevation 57 at the north.

Regrading the Parking Lot

There are several things we know about the parking lot. First, its finish grade may not exceed five percent. Second, the surface water must be drained in the northwest direction, toward the storm drain inlet. Finally, the first revised contour of 61 has been given to us. Therefore, the pattern of revised contours is established by contour 61, and all subsequent contours should be parallel.

With a slope limit of 5 percent (0.05) and a contour interval of one foot, we apply the formula $G = V \div H$, where the gradient G = the vertical component $V \div$ the horizontal component H. Solving for H, we get $H = V \div G$, or $H = 1 \div 0.05 = 20$ feet. Thus, the contours crossing the paved parking area must be 20 feet apart to maintain a uniform 5 percent slope.

Using the same angle established by contour 61, we lay out one-foot contours across the parking area that are exactly 20 feet apart. Because of the vignette design, contour 57 intersects the given spot elevation, and this should send the signal that we are on the right track.

Our next task is to drain the surface water from the land surrounding the paved parking area. We do this by creating swales that begin at the driveway, run along the east and west sides of the parking area, and continue to the storm drain inlet. We begin by drawing flow lines that will act as guides and centerlines for the swale loops. Starting at the uphill part of the site, we reconfigure contour 61 with a loop that runs nearly to the paved driveway. One end of the loop turns north and reconnects with the revised 61 contour running across the paved area. The other end of the loop widens a bit and connects with the existing 61 contour.

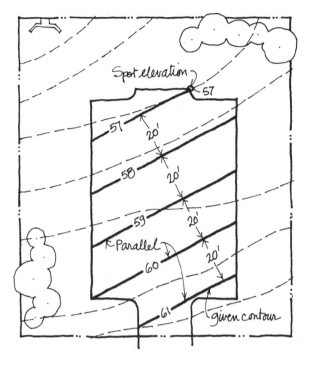

REGRADING THE PARKING LOT

Figure 7.6

We have just created a drainage ditch that will catch the surface water from higher elevations, guide it around the southeast corner of the parking area, and prevent it from flowing across the paved parking area. Our configuration is that of a small valley (contour pointing uphill), and with this first modification, we have set the pattern for the remaining modified contours.

The first loop of the swale on the western side is configured in a similar way. One end of the loop connects with the 60 contour at the southwest corner of the paved area, and the other end of the loop connects with the existing 60 contour near the tree clump at the southwest corner of the site.

The remaining contours on both sides of the parking area are modified in much the same

way as the 60 and 61 contours. Each modification begins where a contour meets the edge of the paved area, loops around the dashed flow line, and reconnects with the same contour. There are two details to keep in mind while completing this exercise. First, you must be certain which contour you are working on, because it is easy to become confused and lose your way. Second, you should maintain a similar distance between the loop ends, so that surface water will flow at a consistent speed.

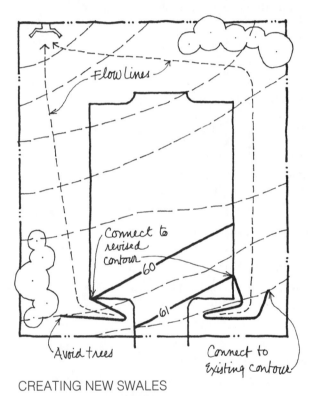

CREATING NEW SWALES

Figure 7.7

Finally, you must verify that no regraded portion of the site exceeds the maximum slope of 20 percent. A 20 percent slope with a contour interval of one foot means that contours should be spaced no closer than five feet apart (G = V ÷ H or 0.20 = 1 ÷ 5). Except for the actual swales themselves, that is, the land within the drainage areas, the appropriate distance has been maintained.

A review of the completed drainage scheme shows the swales conducting water from the highest portion of the site to the storm drain inlet. The rain water that falls on the paved parking area runs in a northwesterly direction toward the same inlet. Therefore, all necessary contours have been modified within the site limits, the surface water has been properly redirected toward the storm drain inlet, and no trees have been affected. Incidentally, the portion of each contour that was not modified is now considered part of the finish contour.

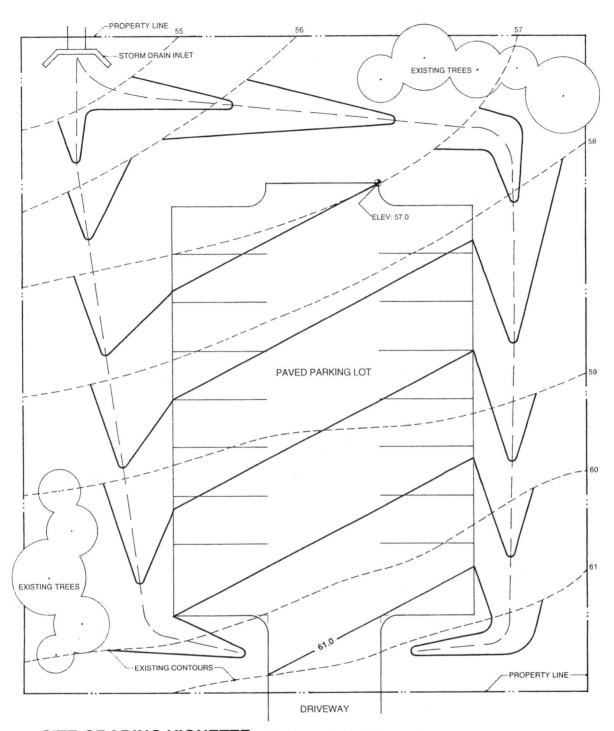

SITE GRADING VIGNETTE - SUGGESTED SOLUTION

Figure 7.8

GLOSSARY

The following glossary defines a number of terms, many of which have appeared on past exams. While this list is by no means complete, it comprises much of the terminology with which candidates should be familiar. You are therefore encouraged to review these definitions as part of your preparation for the exam.

A

Access Right   Right of an owner to have ingress and egress to and from a property.

Accessible Parking   See Handicapped Parking.

Accessory Building   A building or structure on the same lot as the main or principal building.

Aesthetics   The study or theory of beauty.

Air Rights   The rights to the use or control of space above a property.

Altitude   The angle that the sun makes with the horizon.

Aquifer   An underground permeable material through which water flows.

Azimuth   A horizontal angle measured clockwise from north or south.

B

Barrier-Free   The absence of environmental barriers, permitting free access and circulation by the handicapped.

Bearing   In surveying, a direction stated in degrees, minutes, and seconds as an angular deviation east or west from due north or south.

Bearing Capacity   The ability of a soil to support load.

Bench Mark   A relatively permanent point of known location and elevation.

Berm   A convex-shaped bank of earth.

Boundary   The legal recorded property line between two parcels of land.

Buffer Zone   An area separating two different elements or functions.

Buildable Area   The net ground area of a lot that can be covered by a building after required setbacks and other zoning limitations have been accounted for.

Building Line   A defined limit within a property line beyond which a structure may not protrude.

Building Envelope   The enclosure that contains a building's maximum volume.

C

Catch Basin   A drainage device used to collect water, with a deep pit to catch sediment.

Circulation   The flow or movement of people, goods, vehicles, etc., from place to place.

Climate   The generally prevailing weather conditions of a region throughout the year, averaged over a series of years.

Coefficient of Runoff   A fixed ratio of total rainfall that runs off a surface.

Collector Street   A street into which minor streets empty and which leads to a major arterial.

Combined Sewer   Sewer that carries both storm water and sanitary or industrial wastes.

Comfort Zone   Any combination of temperature and humidity in which the average person feels comfortable.

Compaction   The reduction of soil volume by pressure from grading machinery.

Condemnation   Taking private property for public use, with compensation to the owner, under the right of eminent domain.

Conduction   The transfer of heat by direct molecular action.

Conduit Pipe or other channel, below or above ground, for conveying pipelines, cables, or other utilities.

Conforming Use Lawful use of a building or lot that complies with the provisions of the applicable zoning ordinance.

Coniferous Describing a cone-bearing tree or shrub. See Evergreen.

Context The circumstances or elements which surround a particular development.

Contour A line on a plan that connects all points of equal elevation.

Contour Interval The vertical distance between adjacent contour lines.

Convection The transfer of heat by the movement of a liquid or gas, such as air.

Corner Lot A land parcel that fronts on two contiguous streets. The short side is generally considered to be the front of the lot.

Covenant A restriction of the deed which regulates land use, aesthetic qualities, etc., of an area.

Cross Section See Section.

Crown The central area of a convex surface, such as a road.

Cul-De-Sac A short road with an outlet on one end and a turnaround on the other.

Culvert A length of pipe under a road or other barrier used to convey water.

Curb A raised margin running along the edge of a street pavement, usually of concrete.

Curb Cut A depression in a curb that provides vehicular access from a street to a driveway.

Cut and Fill In grading, earth that is removed (cut) or added (fill).

D

Dead-End Parking A circulation layout in which cars are unable to circulate in a continuous one-way flow from the entrance to the exit of a parking area.

Deciduous Describing trees that shed their leaves annually, as opposed to evergreen.

Dedication Appropriation of private property for public use together with acceptance for such use by a public agency.

Deed A written instrument that is used to transfer real property from one party to another.

Degree Days The number of degrees that the mean temperature for any day at a particular location is below 65°F.

Density A measure of the number of people, families, etc., that occupy a specified area.

Discharge Flow from a culvert, sewer, channel, etc.

Disposal Field A system of trenches with gravel and loose pipes through which septic-tank effluent may seep into the surrounding soil. Also called Drainage Field or Absorption Field.

District Any section of a city in which the zoning regulations are uniform.

Drainage (1) The capacity of a soil to receive and transmit water. (2) The system by which excess water is collected, conducted, and dispersed.

Drainage Field See Disposal Field.

Drip Line An imaginary line on the ground described by the outermost branches of a tree.

Driveway A vehicular path generally leading from a public street to a structure on private property.

Drop-Off An area adjacent to a vehicular drive where pedestrians may safely exit (or enter) a car.

Dwelling Unit   An independent living area which includes its own private cooking and bathing facilities.

E

Earthwork   See Grading.

Easement   A limited right, whether temporary or permanent, to use the property of another in a certain way. This may include the right of access to water, light and air, right-of-way, etc.

Ecology   The study of the pattern of relations between organisms and their environment.

Effective Temperature   The sensation produced by the combined effects of temperature, relative humidity, and air movement.

Effluent   Partially treated liquid sewage flowing from any part of a disposal system to a place of final disposition.

Elevation   The vertical distance above sea level or other known point of reference.

Eminent Domain   The right of a government, under the police power concept, to take private property for public use.

Encroachment   Part of a building or an obstruction that extends into the property of another.

Envelope   See Building Envelope.

Environment   The natural and man-made things, conditions, and influences surrounding a person, community, or place.

Erosion   The process by which the surface of the earth is worn away by the action of natural elements, such as water and wind. Also known as Weathering.

Evergreen   Having green leaves throughout the year, as opposed to deciduous.

Excavation   The digging or removal of earth.

Expansive Soil   Clay that swells when wet and shrinks when dried.

F

Finish Floor Level   The completed floor surface on which building occupants walk.

Finish Grade   The elevation of the ground surface after completion of all work.

Floodplain   The land surrounding a flowing stream over which water spreads when a flood occurs.

Floor Area Ratio (FAR)   The ratio of the floor area of a building to the area of the lot.

Flow Line   The path down which water flows.

Front Yard   The minimum legal distance between the front property line and a structure.

Frontage   The length of a lot line along a street or other public way.

Frost Line   The deepest penetration of frost below grade.

Function   The natural or proper purpose for which something is designed or exists.

G

Geology   The science that deals with the physical history of the earth.

Grade   The elevation at any point. See also Gradient and Grading.

Gradient   The rate of slope between two points on a surface, determined by dividing their difference in elevation by their distance apart.

Grading   The modification of earth to create landforms.

Greenbelt   A belt-like area around a city, reserved by ordinance for parkland, farms, open space, etc.

Greenhouse Effect   The direct gain of solar heat, generally through south-facing glass walls and roofs.

Groundwater Level   The plane below which the soil is saturated with water. Also called Groundwater Table or Water Table.

H

Hachure   A shading technique used to depict ground form.

Handicapped   Individuals with physical impairments that result in functional limitations.

Handicapped Parking   Spaces designated for physically handicapped persons, consisting of a typical space with adjacent access aisle no less than five feet wide. Also known as Accessible Parking.

Humidity   The amount or degree of moisture in the air.

Hydrologic Cycle   See Water Cycle.

I

Indigenous   Native to a particular region.

Infiltration   The process by which water soaks into the ground. Also called Percolation.

Insolation   The amount of solar radiation on a given plane.

Interchange   The junction of a freeway with entering or exiting traffic.

Interpolation   Determining an unknown value between known values.

Intersection   The point at which two streets come together or cross.

Invert Elevation   The elevation of the bottom (flow line) of a pipe.

L

Land Coverage   The ratio of the area covered by buildings to the total lot area, expressed as a percentage.

Landscaping   The conscious rearrangement of natural outdoor elements for function and pleasure.

Latitude   The number of degrees north or south of the equator of a particular point on the earth's surface.

Legal Description   Designation of boundaries of real estate in accordance with one of the systems prescribed by law.

Limit Line   Any line beyond which development is prohibited.

Loop Street   A minor street that comes off a major street, runs for a short distance, and then returns to the major street.

Lot Line   The boundary line of a lot.

Lot Area   Total horizontal area within the lot lines of a parcel of land.

M

Macroclimate   The general climate of a region.

Manhole   An access hole in a drainage system to allow inspection, cleaning, and repair.

Metes and Bounds   A formal description of the boundary lines of a parcel of real property in terms of the length and direction of those lines.

Microclimate   The climatic characteristics unique to a small area, caused by local features.

Multiple Dwelling   A building containing three or more dwelling units.

N

Neighborhood   A community of people living in a general vicinity. The area can generally support an elementary school.

Network   A system of circulation channels which covers a large area.

90-Degree Parking   A pattern of vehicle storage in which car stalls are arranged at a right angle to the access lane. Also known as Perpendicular Parking.

Non-Conforming Use   A particular use of land or a structure which is in violation of the applicable zoning code. Generally, if the use was established prior to the code rule which it contravenes, it may continue to exist.

O

Off-Street Parking   Space provided for vehicular parking outside the dedicated street right-of-way.

One-Way Traffic   A circulation system in which all vehicles move in the same direction.

Open Drainage   The removal of unwanted water by means of surface devices.

Orientation   A position with respect to the points of the compass.

P

Pad   An approximately level building area.

Parallel Parking   A pattern of vehicle storage in which car stalls are arranged parallel to the access lane, as in conventional street parking.

Parking Lot   An open space for the storage of motor vehicles.

Parking Stall   A space in a parking lot marked off for the storage of a single motor vehicle.

Party Wall   A wall built on the dividing line between two adjoining parcels, in which each owner has an equal share of ownership.

Passive Solar System   A heating or cooling system that collects and moves solar heat without using mechanical power.

Percolation   See Infiltration.

Perpendicular Parking   See 90-Degree Parking.

Plane Surface   A topographic configuration created by straight, evenly spaced contours.

Planting Strip   A landscaped strip of ground dividing a pedestrian walk from a street.

Police Power   The legal power of a government to authorize actions which are in the best interest of the general public.

Precipitation   Water that falls on the land as rain or snow.

Principal Building   A building that houses the main use or activity occurring on a lot or parcel of ground.

Property Line   A legal boundary of a land parcel.

PUD   A planned unit development, similar to a cluster development but larger in scale including, in addition to housing, commercial and industrial developments.

R

Radiation   The process by which heat or other energy is emitted by a body, transmitted through space, and absorbed by another body.

Rational Method   A method for computing approximate storm water runoff.

Rear Yard   The minimum legal distance between the rear property line and a structure.

Relative Humidity   The ratio of the actual amount of moisture in the air to the maximum amount of moisture the air could hold at a given temperature.

Restrictions   Limitations on the use of property defined by covenant in deeds, by private agreement, or by public legislative action.

Retaining Wall   A wall constructed of timber, masonry, or concrete designed to resist the pressure of the earth mass with which it is in contact.

Retention Pond   An area used to retain and hold runoff water during a storm. The water is held until it is able to drain naturally.

Ridge   A narrow convex land configuration represented by contours pointing downhill.

Right-Of-Way   A strip of land granted by deed or easement for a circulation path.

Runoff   The surface flow of water from an area.

S

Section   The representation of a structure as it would appear if cut through by an intersecting plane to show its internal configuration. Also known as a Cross Section.

Septic System   A sewage treatment system consisting of a tank and filtering system.

Setback   The minimum legal distance between a property line and a structure.

Sewer   An underground pipe or drain used to carry off excess water and waste matter.

Sheeting   A thin layer of water moving across a surface. Also called Sheet Flow.

Side Yard   The minimum legal distance between side property lines and a structure.

Silt   A fine-grained soil whose particles are 0.05 to 0.002 millimeters in diameter.

Site Planning   The art or science of creating or arranging the external physical environment.

Slope   The inclination of a surface expressed as a percentage or proportion.

Sludge   Accumulated solids that settle out of the sewage, forming a semi-liquid mass on the bottom of a septic tank.

Soil   A natural material, formed of decomposed and disintegrated parent rock, that supports plant life.

Soil Boring Log   A graphic representation of the soils encountered in a test boring.

Solar Zoning   An ordinance controlling the mass and shape of buildings, which permits the penetration of sunlight between buildings.

Split Lot   A lot that comprises more than one zone.

Spot Elevation   The exact elevation at a key point on the ground or on a structure.

Spot Zoning   Zoning that differs from the pattern of the surrounding area.

Stall   See Parking Stall.

Story   The vertical portion of a building included between the surface of any floor and the surface of the floor next above.

Subsidence   The sinking of land.

Summit   The highest point of a land mass, represented by concentric contours.

Sun Chart   A map of the sky showing the path of the sun, from sunrise to sunset, on the 21st day of each month.

Surcharge   Earth which is above the top of a retaining wall level.

Surface Water   Water that runs along the surface of the ground, as opposed to below ground.

Swale   A graded flow path used in open drainage systems.

Switchback Road   A road that doubles back on itself with a hairpin curve.

T

Topography   The configuration of the earth's surface.

Topsoil   The upper six to eight inches of soil, which contains humus.

Transpiration   The process by which water vapor escapes into the atmosphere from plants.

Trench Drain   A linear drainage device used to collect and conduct water.

U

Uniform Slope   A topographic configuration created by evenly spaced contours.

Utility Easement   A legal right-of-way enabling a utility company to run service lines over private property.

V

Valley   A narrow concave land configuration represented by contours pointing uphill.

Variance   The special permission granted to the owner of a parcel of land waiving certain specific restrictions when the enforcement of these would impose an unusual or unreasonable hardship on the owner.

Vegetation   All the plants, shrubs, and trees of a particular place.

W

Water Cycle   The general pattern of movement of the water on, under, and above the earth. Also called Hydrologic Cycle.

Water Table   See Groundwater Level.

Way   Street, alley, or other thoroughfare or easement permanently established for passage of persons or vehicles.

Weathering   See Erosion.

Windbreak   A structure or plant which, because of its form and location, reduces wind velocities.

Wind Shadow   The area near the bottom of the leeward side of a hill, where the wind velocity decreases to almost zero.

Y

Yard   Open, unoccupied space on all sides of a building, based on the required setbacks.

Z

Zone   Area established by a governing body for specific use, such as residential, commercial, or industrial use.

Zone of Aeration   The zone below the ground in which the spaces between soil grains contain both water and air.

Zone of Saturation   The zone below the ground in which all of the spaces between soil grains are filled completely with water.

Zoning   The legal means whereby land use is regulated and controlled for the general welfare.

Zoning Ordinance   Exercise of police power by a government in regulating and controlling the character and use of property.

BIBLIOGRAPHY

The following list of books is provided for candidates who may wish to do further research or study in Site Planning & Design. Most of the b1ooks listed below are available in college or technical bookstores, and all would

ANSI A117.1 Handicapped Standards
American National Standards Institute
New York, NY

Architectural Graphic Standards
Ramsey and Sleeper
John Wiley & Sons, Inc.
New York, NY

Basic Elements of Landscape Architectural Design
Booth, Norman K.
Elsevier Science Publishing Co.
New York, NY

Design with Climate
Olgyay, Victor
Princeton University Press
Princeton, NJ

Environmental Analysis
Marsh, William M.
McGraw-Hill Book Co.
New York, NY

Landscape Architecture
Simonds, John O.
McGraw-Hill Book Co.
New York, NY

Landscape Planning for Energy Conservation
Environmental Design Press
Reston, VA

Principles & Practices of Grading, Drainage, and Road Alignment
Untermann, Richard K.
Reston Publishing Co.
Reston, VA

make welcome additions to any architectural bookshelf. In addition to the course material and the volumes listed below, we advise candidates to review regularly the many professional journals, which are available at most architectural offices.

Site Planning
Lynch, Kevin
M.I.T. Press
Cambridge, MA

Site Planning Standards
De Chiara, Joseph
McGraw-Hill Publishing Co.
New York, NY

Solar Dwelling Design Concepts
AIA Research Corporation
Washington, DC

The Passive Solar Energy Book
Mazria, Edward
Rodale Press
Emmaus, PA

The Urban Pattern
Gallion, Arthur B.
Van Nostrand Co.
New York, NY

Time Saver Standards for Site Planning
DeChiara/Koppelman
Van Nostrand Reinhold Co.
New York, NY

Urban Design
Spreiregen, Paul D.
McGraw-Hill Book Co.
New York, NY

The Architect's Studio Companion: Rules of Thumb for Preliminary Design
John Wiley & Sons, Inc.
New York, NY

*Design on the Land: The Development of
Landscape Architecture*
Belknap Press
New York, NY

Grade Easy
Landscape Architecture Foundation

Simplified Site Engineering
John Wiley & Sons, Inc.
New York, NY

Lesson One

1. C   See page 5.

2. B   See discussion of freeways on page 6.

3. D   See page 1.

4. B   60-degree parking is not as efficient, safe, or cost-effective as 90-degree parking; however, it is easier for a driver to use than 90-degree parking.

5. A   All of the other choices would create congestion or safety hazards.

6. B   In street design, compound curves (II) should generally be avoided, and parking lanes (IV) should be included, where feasible, because of their convenience.

7. C   Power lines below ground are better than above-ground lines in almost every way, except cost.

8. D   The minimum space required to turn a wheelchair is a circle five feet in diameter. See pages 18 and 19.

9. A   Level paved areas (III) cause ponding of water, and dead end aisles (IV) create unnecessary traffic congestion. See page 13.

10. C   All the choices are desirable objectives of pedestrian circulation, but safety is primary. See page 14.

Lesson Two

1. C   Subsurface water should be diverted away from a building's foundation by means of drainage tiles laid in a gravel bed. Foundations should be placed above, not below, the water table (A), and contours are modified during rough, not finish, grading (B).

2. A   A mat footing distributes vertical loads over the entire building area and is used when soil conditions are poor.

3. D   When upper soils have low bearing capacity, piles may be used to transmit a building's loads to deeper, firmer soils.

4. D   See page 53.

5. D   Boat footings are used where the underlying soil has a low bearing capacity, jetted piles are rarely used, and wood piles are used for light to moderate loads. The only appropriate choice is structural steel piles.

6. C   As load is placed on a footing, it compresses the soil and reduces the soil's void volume. Although this results in settlement, it is not necessarily differential settlement.

7. B   This is a question in which all the answers are at least partially correct. However, the most inclusive answer is B, to determine the character of the soil.

8. C   If design for a 5-year storm is found to be inadequate, one must design for a more severe storm, such as one that would likely occur every 10 years. Designing for a 100-year storm would be excessively cautious, while using a subsurface system or non-erosive materials would not necessarily handle a greater amount of runoff.

9. D   Roof slopes and eave widths are irrelevant, because during a storm, the same amount of water eventually drains off all roof areas. However, runoff may be reduced by using greater areas of vegetation that permit storm water to seep into the ground.

10. B   Topography is the shape of the ground surface, not an element of climate.

Lesson Three

1. **D** All of the above. The holistic approach to sustainably designed projects encourages the design team to examine the impact of environmental, economic, mechanical, and aesthetic architectural decisions.

2. **D** None of the above.

   Choice I is not correct. The zone of the earth that supports human life (five miles into the earth's crust and five miles into the atmosphere) is an extremely fragile ecosystem. This biosphere that has evolved over millions of years has been dramatically affected by the growth of human activity in the last 150 years.

   Choice II is not correct either. While innovative technologies are improving energy efficiency of some building systems, the vast majority of the built environment is energy inefficient.

   Choice III is also not correct. Toxic substances have the tendency to expand and affect large areas. For example, the air above the Great Lakes contains evidence of DDT, a toxic pesticide banned in the United States decades ago. It was discovered that DDT is captured in the jet stream bringing toxic materials from far away continents, which still use toxic pesticides.

   Choice IV is not correct. While recycling is helpful, it is just the beginning of the sustainable design process. The principles of sustainable design say that we need to have more building products that can be recycled and are biodegradable to create a more sustainable ecosystem.

3. **C** I, III, and IV

   Choice I is correct. Designing with native landscaping is preferred to using exotic or imported plant types. Indigenous plants tend to survive longer, use less water, and cost less.

   Choice II is not correct. Placing any structure in a floodplain, even those that resist floodwater, is not desirable. Placing buildings in a floodplain can increase flooding farther down stream.

   Choice III is also correct. Buildings sensitive to the benefits of solar orientation and passive and active solar gain techniques save energy and are more visually aligned with local climatic conditions.

   Choice IV is correct as well. In-fill development and proximity to a variety of transportation options are design principles that benefit the inhabitants and their environment.

4. **C** III and IV

   I is not correct. Communities that are only residential are not encouraged. Mixed-use development (combining housing, retail, open space, and commercial) is a preferred sustainable design.

   II is not correct. Open space should not be designed only for recreation and wildlife habitat. Additional uses such as environmental education, storm water retention, flood control, wetlands drainage, and so on, should be considered in sustainable planning.

   III is correct. The Ahwahnee principles support a wide range of interconnected transportation to encourage many options for travel.

   IV is also correct. Development that permits opportunities for a diverse number of jobs is a key goal of the Ahwahnee Principles.

5. **D** All of the above

   I is correct. While first cost is not the primary concern of life cycle costing, it is one of the economic factors considered.

   II is also correct. The cost of maintenance is part of the evaluation.

III is correct as well. The durability of a product or system is considered in the cost of repair and part of the overall evaluation.

IV is correct because the comparison of product or system life is one of the factors evaluated in life cycle costing.

6. B   I, II, and III

I is correct. LEED has several options for improving IAQ (Indoor Air Quality) including filtering the air system and installing low VOC (Volatile Organic Compound) paints and caulking.

II is also correct. Methods to store, recirculate, and locally distribute rainwater are encouraged.

III is correct as well. Innovative solutions to energy conservation such as fuel cells, photovoltaic panels, and gas turbine energy production are encouraged in the LEED accreditation system.

IV is incorrect. Unfortunately, the LEED system awards no points awards for designs with strong aesthetics.

7. D   All of the above

All of these consultants (wetlands engineer, energy commissioner, landscape architect, and energy modeling engineer) might be necessary for the holistic approach to sustainable design. The landscape architect should have experience with local, native plant design.

8. C   I, II, and IV

I is correct. Computer programs that allow energy modeling of design options allow the architect a quick method of evaluating numerous different solutions.

II is also correct. It is extremely important that the client be able to understand the value of sustainable design solutions.

III is not correct. Art selection is at the client's discretion.

IV is correct. Locating the most energy efficient appliances, plumbing fixtures, and office equipment will improve the energy efficiency of the entire project.

9. B   I, III, and IV

I is correct. Solar orientation can affect many architectural design elements including massing, landscaping, fenestration, and building skin design.

II is not correct. Landscape design should be functional as well as visually pleasing. Landscape design for purely visual impact is not consistent with the sustainable design approach.

III is also correct. Architectural design that understands the context (scale, color, style, texture) of adjacent structures is sympathetic to the sustainable design philosophy.

IV is correct as well. Understanding all site conditions, and their potential to assist building's energy systems is helpful. For example, ground water connected to a heat pump is a good source of supplemental energy for cooling and heating a building.

10. A   I, II, and IV

I is correct. Solar shading, whether from landscaping or architectural elements, can regulate the insulation to increase winter light and reduce warm summer sunlight.

II is also correct. Urban heat island effect is the tendency of a building roof to absorb solar radiation during the day and then emit heat radiation during the evening. Roof systems with grass or light colored roofing material reduce the urban heat island effect.

III is not correct. Sustainable design encourages approaches that reduce the area allocated to parking.

IV is correct. The type, location, and size of building fenestration are key aspects of architectural design for sustainable projects.

The examination on the following pages should be taken when you have completed your study of all the lessons in this course. It is designed to simulate the Site Planning & Design division of the Architect Registration Examination. Many questions are intentionally difficult in order to reflect the pattern of questions you may expect to encounter on the actual examination.

You will also notice that the subject matter for several questions has not been covered in the course material. This situation is inevitable and, thus, should provide you with practice in making an educated guess. Other questions may appear ambiguous, trivial, or simply unfair. This too, unfortunately, reflects the actual experience of the exam and should prepare you for the worst you may encounter.

Answers and complete explanations will be found on the pages following the examination, to permit self-grading. **Do not look at these answers until you have completed the entire exam.** Once the examination is completed and graded, your weaknesses will be revealed, and you are urged to do further study in those areas.

Please observe the following directions:

1. The examination is closed book; please do not use any reference material.

2. Allow about one hour to answer all questions. Time is definitely a factor to be seriously considered.

3. Read all questions *carefully* and mark the appropriate answer on the answer sheet provided.

4. Answer all questions, even if you must guess. Do not leave any questions unanswered.

5. If time allows, review your answers, but do not arbitrarily change any answer.

6. Turn to the answers only after you have completed the entire examination.

GOOD LUCK!

EXAMINATION ANSWER SHEET

Directions: Read each question and its lettered answers. When you have decided which answer is correct, blacken the corresponding space on this sheet. After completing the exam, you may grade yourself; complete answers and explanations will be found on the pages following the examination.

1. Ⓐ Ⓑ Ⓒ Ⓓ
2. Ⓐ Ⓑ Ⓒ Ⓓ
3. Ⓐ Ⓑ Ⓒ Ⓓ
4. Ⓐ Ⓑ Ⓒ Ⓓ
5. Ⓐ Ⓑ Ⓒ Ⓓ
6. Ⓐ Ⓑ Ⓒ Ⓓ
7. Ⓐ Ⓑ Ⓒ Ⓓ
8. Ⓐ Ⓑ Ⓒ Ⓓ
9. Ⓐ Ⓑ Ⓒ Ⓓ
10. Ⓐ Ⓑ Ⓒ Ⓓ
11. Ⓐ Ⓑ Ⓒ Ⓓ
12. Ⓐ Ⓑ Ⓒ Ⓓ
13. Ⓐ Ⓑ Ⓒ Ⓓ
14. Ⓐ Ⓑ Ⓒ Ⓓ
15. Ⓐ Ⓑ Ⓒ Ⓓ
16. Ⓐ Ⓑ Ⓒ Ⓓ
17. Ⓐ Ⓑ Ⓒ Ⓓ
18. Ⓐ Ⓑ Ⓒ Ⓓ

19. Ⓐ Ⓑ Ⓒ Ⓓ
20. Ⓐ Ⓑ Ⓒ Ⓓ
21. Ⓐ Ⓑ Ⓒ Ⓓ
22. Ⓐ Ⓑ Ⓒ Ⓓ
23. Ⓐ Ⓑ Ⓒ Ⓓ
24. Ⓐ Ⓑ Ⓒ Ⓓ
25. Ⓐ Ⓑ Ⓒ Ⓓ
26. Ⓐ Ⓑ Ⓒ Ⓓ
27. Ⓐ Ⓑ Ⓒ Ⓓ
28. Ⓐ Ⓑ Ⓒ Ⓓ
29. Ⓐ Ⓑ Ⓒ Ⓓ
30. Ⓐ Ⓑ Ⓒ Ⓓ
31. Ⓐ Ⓑ Ⓒ Ⓓ
32. Ⓐ Ⓑ Ⓒ Ⓓ
33. Ⓐ Ⓑ Ⓒ Ⓓ
34. Ⓐ Ⓑ Ⓒ Ⓓ
35. Ⓐ Ⓑ Ⓒ Ⓓ

1. The number of test borings that should be drilled on a particular site is determined by all of the following, EXCEPT

    A. the uniformity of the subsurface conditions.

    B. the complexity of the building footprint.

    C. the ground floor area of the proposed building.

    D. the depth at which firm strata are encountered.

2. If an open entrance plaza is on the wind-ward side of a high-rise building, the plaza may be sheltered from the wind by

    A. planting a row of closely spaced deciduous trees adjacent to the plaza.

    B. planting a row of closely spaced ever-green trees adjacent to the plaza.

    C. building a six-foot-high masonry wall adjacent to the plaza.

    D. relocating the entrance plaza to the leeward side of the building.

3. The most effective way to reduce the consequences of vandalism would be to employ

    A. exterior floodlighting.

    B. trained guard dogs.

    C. impact-resistant materials.

    D. burglar alarm systems.

4. An aquifer is

    A. a surface soil that experiences heavy runoff.

    B. an underground permeable material through that water flows.

    C. the boundary between the zone of aeration and the zone of saturation.

    D. the boundary between soil layers, along which sliding may occur.

5. Materials with high heat-storage values would be most appropriate to use in

    A. Phoenix, Arizona.

    B. Honolulu, Hawaii.

    C. Miami, Florida.

    D. Houston, Texas.

6. Compared to conventional foundations, pile foundations

    I.   are more costly.

    II. are more permanent.

    III. employ a wider range of materials.

    IV. support greater building loads.

    V.   can be constructed more quickly.

    A. I and IV   C. II, III, and V

    B. I and III   D. I, III, and IV

7. Legal restrictions that are imposed on land by private parties are known as

    A. ordinances.

    B. conditional uses.

    C. variances.

    D. deed restrictions

8. Which of the following is NOT a consequence of zoning ordinances?

    A. Limited population density

    B. Segregated permitted uses

    C. Restricted lot coverage

    D. Diminished fire danger

9. Referring to the plan shown below, what are the are the correct values of dimensions 1, 2, and 3?

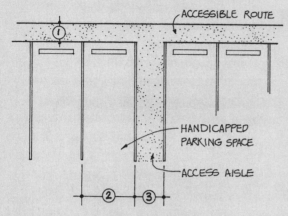

ACCESSIBLE ROUTE

HANDICAPPED PARKING SPACE

ACCESS AISLE

A. 3' - 0", 8' - 0", 3' - 0"

B. 3' - 0", 8' - 0", 5' - 0"

C. 3' - 6", 8' - 6", 5' - 6"

D. 4' - 0", 9' - 0", 4' - 0"

10. The type and size of a shopping center is primarily determined by its catchment area, which is defined as the area

   A. from which it derives its user population.

   B. within a 30-minute driving radius of the shopping center.

   C. housing a sufficient user population to make the facility viable.

   D. necessary to situate a major department store and its required parking.

11. The sun chart for a specific latitude reveals which of the following?

   I.   The sun's altitude

   II. The sun's azimuth

   III. The amount of sunshine

   IV. The number of degree days

   V.   The time of sunrise

   A. I and III   C. I, II, and V

   B. II and V   D. I, IV, and V

12. On a moderate hillside that rises behind a housing development, one could reduce the need for a complex drainage system by

   A. paving the hillside area with an impervious material.

   B. grading level areas into the hillside.

   C. providing a thick ground cover of plant material.

   D. creating earth berms at the foot of the slope.

13. Which of the following organizational forms would be best suited to a large, low-cost housing development if the primary concern were cost?

   A. Linear

   B. Radial

   C. Compact

   D. Decentralized

14. Which organizational pattern BEST describes the configuration of a conventional suburban shopping mall?

   A. Axial

   B. Linear

   C. Grid

   D. Radial

15. Which organizational pattern formed the basis of development in ancient, classical Rome?

   A. Linear

   B. Precinctual

   C. Grid

   D. Ring

16. Which of the following does NOT directly impose legal constraints on the proposed development of land?

    A. Deed restrictions

    B. Zoning ordinances

    C. Easements

    D. Environmental impact statements

17. The amount of solar radiation received by a site is influenced by the site's

I. slope.	**III.** wind patterns.
II. latitude.	**IV.** longitude.
A. I and II	**C.** I and III
B. II and IV	**D.** II and III

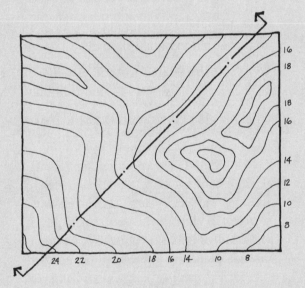

18. Which of the topographic profiles shown below correctly represents the section cut through the plan at left?

A.

B.

C.

D.

19. Which of the following facts is NOT relevant for analyzing the orientation of a new building on a particular site?

    A. Neighboring buildings to the west are supported on piers drilled into bedrock.

    B. Prevailing winds are from the southwest.

    C. The greatest source of noise is an expressway to the east.

    D. The new building is to be heated partially by solar energy.

20. A site slopes up from the street five feet for every 20 feet of horizontal distance. In order to use this site for parking cars, the site

    A. may be used as is.

    B. must be regraded to 1.5 in 10.

    C. must be regraded to 1 in 10.

    D. must be regraded to 0.5 in 10.

21. Compared to a site containing a large amount of loose silt, a site with a similar amount of organic soil would be

  A. more costly to develop.

  B. less costly to develop.

  C. similar in cost to develop.

  D. too costly to develop.

22. If an architect is presented with a sloping site with large areas of loose fill, and the client wishes to develop this site for an elementary school, the architect should

  A. reject the site because schools require level land.

  B. reject the site because of inadequate soil-bearing value.

  C. reject the site because development costs will be excessive.

  D. attempt to find a solution using the site's unique properties.

23. Which of the following measures would help reduce automobile usage, and hence congestion, in the development of an office building in a central city area?

  I. Provide low-rate parking in the building, with free parking for all tenants and their staffs.

  II. Provide only market-rate monthly parking.

  III. Provide no parking (or limited parking) with a tax system in which a portion of the real estate tax on the building is earmarked for public transit.

  IV. Provide incentive rates for tenants and their staffs who car pool.

  A. I and II   **C.** I and IV

  B. II, III, and IV   **D.** II and IV

24. In analyzing a building site, which of the following conditions would indicate the probability of poor drainage?

  I. Existing dense ground cover

  II. Existing flowing stream

  III. Existing high water table

  IV. Relatively flat site

  V. No storm drainage system

  A. I and II   **C.** II, III, and IV

  B. III, IV, and V   **D.** I, III, and V

25. Compared to a town located at the base of a mountain, the summer temperature of a mountain resort 3,000 feet above the town would be

  A. cooler at all times.

  B. cooler in the higher latitudes.

  C. warmer by day and cooler by night.

  D. generally the same.

26. Under normal conditions, a steady slope of 10 percent is a desirable limit for which of the following?

  I. Storm drainage flow

  II. Pedestrian walks

  III. Planted banks

  IV. Unretained earth cuts

  V. Drainage ditches

  A. II and V   **C.** I, II, and V

  B. II and III   **D.** I, III, and IV

27. Compared to a developed urban area, a planted rural area will

  A. reduce the normal amount of rainfall.

  B. reduce wind velocities.

  C. purify the air of harmful pollutants.

  D. stabilize the microclimate.